'I devoured this correspondence between Sue and Bruce. It has all the humour and metaphors you could wish for in an intimate exchange about the angst of ever getting a film made, anywhere, any time. Also embedded in the text is the importance of maintaining our screen archive. This funny, informative exchange is a lesson in high-wire acts for any would-be filmmaker.'

Margaret Pomeranz

'In touch with each other by fax while they flew all over the world, two brilliant Australians left a sparkling record of how they lived and worked as the film business turned into the international country we know today. Milliken emerges as the ideally wise and funny producer, while Beresford's wide-ranging curiosity makes you wonder how much more famous he would now be as a director if he had only put "A Film by Bruce Beresford" on the front of pictures like *Black Robe*. But he was too modest for that, or perhaps just insufficiently insane.'

Clive James

'Loved this. Like a Stop, Detour or Danger sign for any unsuspecting filmmaker. Succour to know even Bruce Beresford has this many obstacles to surmount getting a film green lit. But how blessed he was to have Sue fighting like a tiger in his corner, supporting his vision, defeating the obstacles and reporting back on the local scene with such perception and wit. Read it like a survival manual for a career in filmmaking. Or die.'

Rachel Ward

'Two of Australia's most successful practitioners react with wry resignation, indomitable fortitude, and high-speed improvisation to get cameras rolling, as deals collapse at the eleventh hour and stars go feral. Required reading if you have any illusions about the glamour of filmmaking.'

David Williamson

'Often funny, always revealing, a compelling journey into the bi-polar world of filmmaking, its capricious uncertainties vividly chronicled in the correspondence between two collaborators navigating their way through the labyrinth. It is also the story of the enduring friendship which helped them do so.'

Al Clark

31/8/91

To Sue MILLIKEN

Dear Sue,

Belinda's poster just arrived & I think it's very good. The single image is arresting and stylish. Virginia said " Oh it's just a pictrue of a priest, who'll want to see that"? BUT it is selling the film we've made & I believe that's important.

I also think the catchphrase is effective - ironic.

See you on thursday in Toronto. Smart thinking of you to keep chasing them up about the cinema & projection. Is the print they're showing one done in a Canadian lab? If so, we could be in trouble. Should we ship over an Australian print as a back up?

Will you bring a big jar of vegemite?

Also, there's a new book out on Jeffrey Smart. If you have time could you get it for me as I want it as a present for someone.

Love,

Bruce

There's a Fax from Bruce

Edited correspondence between
Director Bruce Beresford
and Producer Sue Milliken
October 1989 to March 1996

FOREWORD BY
ANTHONY BUCKLEY AM

Currency Press, Sydney

First published in 2016 by
Currency Press Pty Ltd
PO Box 2287, Strawberry Hills
NSW 2012 Australia
enquiries@currency.com.au
www.currency.com.au

Cataloguing-in-Publication data for this title is available from the National Library of Australia website: www.nla.gov.au

Cover design by Lisa White for Currency Press.

Index by Alan Walker.

Currency Press acknowledges the Traditional Owners of the Country on which we live and work. We pay our respects to all Aboriginal and Torres Strait Islander Elders, past and present.

FOREWORD
ANTHONY BUCKLEY

Receiving a fax from Bruce Beresford first thing in the morning generally guarantees a good start to the day. No matter how serious the subject, or the enquiry, one can be sure it will be liberally laced with laconic or sardonic wit and humour for the addressee's eyes only. Sue Milliken's responses are equally pithy and wryly observant. This exchange of faxes guarantees a great read.

Most people have an idea of what movie making is about. The director tells the actors what to do, the make-up artist applies the make-up to their faces, the costume designer dresses them, while the sound man records what they have to say. But what on earth does the producer do?

Well for a start, none of these people would have a job without a producer.

Kenneth Macgowan, in his 1965 publication *Behind the Screen – The History and Techniques of the Motion Picture*, only devotes one page of his volume to what a producer does, and sums it up rather pithily. A producer used to be

> a man [no women in 1965!] who asks a studio employee a question, gives him the answer, and tells him he is wrong... At his worst, the producer may be a frightened fellow who keeps his eye on the past and tries to turn out the sort of films that made money last year. [Hollywood is still doing this!] At his best, the producer has real creative power. He can recognise a good story that doesn't follow a cyclic pattern or any current formula. He can see how such a story

> must be handled to make an effective contribution to the progress of the screen and the profits of the business. He can bring to it the writer and the director who will be sympathetic to the material, and capable of getting the most out of it.

Mr Macgowan's words are sage advice indeed, as herein lies the secret of producing – bringing together the people who will make a success of making it happen.

I don't believe anyone sets out to make a bad picture, but they do happen because movie making invites people whose ambition far outweighs their abilities. I think the prerogative of casting the picture is very much the director's, but I see the producer's role as making sure the director is surrounded by the very best people to facilitate his or her wishes, and I surround myself with people who know far more than I do. In my career I regret to say I have seen too many of my peers fail because they have surrounded themselves with people lesser than themselves.

This treasure lode of faxes reveals an aspect of the picture making business that I have not come across before. You can read all the textbooks in the world but they won't teach you the realities that these faxes reveal, of the importance of the relationship between the director and producer. Each is dependent on the other if the producer is doing their job properly. If the director has made a request, the director is entitled to the decision from the producer, then and there, it cannot wait till tomorrow. Sue Milliken sets a fine example of making decisions then and there. However, raising the money for a picture is fraught with frustration and occasionally despair and it never gets any easier.

At a crowded assembly at the Film School at North Ryde some years ago, I heard Peter Weir describe the director as 'the captain of the ship'. 'Ah,' I muttered, 'but the producer is the commodore of the line.'

Enjoy the read and, yes, you will wonder why we do it.

Anthony Buckley A.M.
Sydney, January 2016

CONTENTS

For Greg Coote and Richard Zanuck

BACKGROUND
SUE MILLIKEN

In the 1980s, Bruce Beresford and I were in mid-career in a world which welcomed movie makers. The Australian film industry had reinvented itself in the 1970s, and Beresford had been one of the earliest talents to emerge from that renaissance. He made seven Australian feature films including *The Getting of Wisdom* and *Breaker Morant* before beginning a career in the US that made him internationally famous, with a string of successful films including *Tender Mercies* and the Oscar-winning *Driving Miss Daisy.*

Meanwhile, I had been building my own, more parochial, career in Australian films, firstly in production as a continuity girl and production manager, and with my then husband Tom Jeffrey as a producer. Among the films we produced was the Vietnam movie, *The Odd Angry Shot.*

In 1980 I was asked to set up the Australian operation of the international completion bond company Film Finances. From then on I managed the business in Australia and New Zealand and, with the tacit agreement of the head of Film Finances, Richard Soames, I continued to produce my own films.

In 1985 Bruce returned home to make a film of Nene Gare's novel *The Fringe Dwellers,* about Aboriginal people striving for a better life. He had found distribution interest in the UK but he needed an Australian producer to complete the financing and to oversee the production. Prior to this I knew him only slightly, but now we met and he invited me to produce the film for him. Serendipitously this brought me together with a director whose work I greatly admired and a subject I believed was of groundbreaking and timely importance. The film won a number of awards and went on to be Australia's entry in Competition at the Cannes Film Festival in 1986.

For the next ten years, while pursuing our individual lives, we worked on developing Australian films, some of which, in the way of the industry, never made it to the first day of shooting. As Bruce was out of the country for a large part of the time, we communicated via the latest technical innovation, the fax machine. Because of the time difference, I could write a fax to Bruce at the end of my day in Sydney, and he would reply at the end of his day in Los Angeles or London, which meant that most mornings when I arrived in the office, my assistant Chris Gordon would announce: 'There's a fax from Bruce.'

Because Bruce, his wife Virginia Duigan and their young daughter Trilby were away for long periods, I tried where possible to include in my faxes news, film industry gossip and other events I thought might interest and entertain them. Bruce's faxes were mostly about the matters at hand, but they sometimes ruminated on films he had seen, or books he had read or the bizarre behaviour of some of the more eccentric members of the international film community. Bruce's adult children from his first marriage to Rhoisin – Benjamin, Cordelia and Adam – were living mostly in the UK and he spent as much time with them as he could in between, or sometimes during, his work on his films.

After *The Fringe Dwellers* we took an option on a script based on the true story of an entombed miner in Kalgoorlie in 1908 titled *The End of the Line*. The legendary Italian producer Dino De Laurentiis was a great fan of Bruce's, and when he came to set up an Australian production company, he offered to finance the film. But without warning when the contracting was almost completed, Dino switched Bruce on to a project he wanted to make at his new studios in

Queensland, called *Total Recall.* I went along as the film's producer. What followed was a year of pre-production which eventually went nowhere when the De Laurentiis empire collapsed in the world financial crash of 1987, taking the film with it. *Total Recall* was sold to a US company, which made it into an international hit starring Arnold Schwarzenegger.

For the next three years Bruce worked in Hollywood. I produced a movie for television and continued to work on the development of various projects and on my day job, managing Film Finances in Australia.

During this time Bruce read the novel *Black Robe.* The author, Brian Moore, put him in touch with Canadian producer Robert Lantos, who set out to finance a film adaptation with Bruce directing. Set in the seventeenth century, *Black Robe* is about the clash of cultures between proselytising French Jesuit missionaries and the indigenous people of northern Canada, and the crisis of faith of a priest, Father Laforgue.

Problems with the financing led to my being asked to help put the film together as a Canadian–Australian co-production, and to act as the Australian producer. But because *Black Robe* was not an Australian story and filming would take place in Canada, the Australian government funding body of the day, the Australian Film Finance Corporation (FFC), was wary of contributing. On one level this was understandable as it had just taken a lot of flak for investing in Peter Weir's *Green Card*, which starred Gérard Depardieu and was filmed in France (and which ironically was to become the FFC's biggest profit-maker). Both films, however, were official government-to-government co-productions, the purpose of which was to enable small film industries to co-operate with each other to compete with Hollywood. As such we were entitled to seek FFC investment.

This book begins during the financing of *Black Robe.* The correspondence is suspended while the film was being made, as we were together on location and then in Sydney during post-production. It recommences when Bruce is once again in the US, preparing to direct *Rich in Love*, and it continues more or less uninterrupted until we began pre-production for *Paradise Road* in Sydney in 1996. In between, Bruce directed four films and squeezed in a couple of operas – *Elektra* for the State Opera of South Australia and *Sweeney Todd* for Portland Opera.

In addition to developing films and overseeing Film Finances' activities, I produced two features during this period, *Sirens* and *Dating the Enemy*. At the same time I was involved with a number of film industry organisations: I was on the Council of the Screen Producers Association of Australia (SPAA) and in 1993 was appointed as a member, and then chair, of the Australian Film Commission (AFC), which oversaw film development and culture. I was also a member of the Board of Review at the Office of Film & Literature Classification, which heard censorship appeals by film distributors.

Bruce never stopped wanting to make Australian films and he took a close interest in what was going on, as I tried both to bring our projects to production and to make sure that he would actually be available if and when the money came together – the latter the cause of considerable anxiety as he cheerfully accepted one Hollywood picture after another.

We both shared a love of skiing, although we almost never got to the mountains at the same time. Directors always have to be on the spot, so Bruce's plans were constantly frustrated. With the invention of the fax, which made communication so easy, I discovered that producers can, some of the time, work from anywhere. Many a day on the slopes was followed by hours on the phone to the office, dictating replies to the pile of faxes awaiting me at reception, while my pals worked their way through a jug of margaritas. But I did get that priceless time on the mountain, when all that mattered was the pristine beauty of the surroundings and the challenge of staying upright at high speed.

Another lifeline to sanity was the dogs; first Rita the Wonder Dog, so named because she was a talented actor, and on her departure to a better life, Jess the blue heeler. We took the dog to the office, which not only meant that the dog spent the day in convivial company but that the workers had someone to pat when the pressure got to breaking point.

Throughout these years, the patient and saintly Chris Gordon managed the chaos, fed the dog when a long day meant a late dinner, and kept track of my life. More than ten years later, after her unfairly early death from cancer, I came across a storage box titled Sue's Files. That box has become this book.

Making films is a business which combines dreams with large amounts of money. And not even your own money, someone else's money. What could be more fun than that? Still, it is harder than it looks, as what follows will demonstrate.

Sue Milliken,
Sydney, March 2016

CHAPTER ONE: 1989–91

A journey to paradise

FAX FROM Bruce to Sue, 8 October 1989
211 N. Bronson, Los Angeles CA

Dear Sue

Thanks for the *Black Robe* fax. I guess we'll have to look for Daniel in Australia, as there is no Laforgue unless Sam Neill (who would be fine) is acceptable to the financiers. Bryan Brown wouldn't be right for the role, and nor would Mel Gibson even if we could afford him, which we can't.

I'll be in Nigeria from the end of October, though for quite a bit of November I'll be in London casting *Mister Johnson*. Then I'll be back in London from March, so it's not as if I'm marching off never to be seen again.

Virginia will be in Sydney around 16 October and will call you.

Lots of love,
Bruce

FAX FROM Sue to Bruce, 17 October 1989

Dear Bruce

Herewith a letter to Alliance [the Canadian production company] about *Black Robe*. Are they thick or what? I've told them in every communication that the Australian lead actor is essential to the deal, and they still keep asking!

What do you think of the idea of Liz Mullinar and I doing a casting tape of the boy? If we had a couple of weeks we could put down most of the likely contenders, which might allay everyone's concerns – or the opposite.

Cheers,
Sue

FAX FROM Sue to Bruce, 17 November 1989

Dear Bruce

Attached is another in the continuing tennis match of correspondence regarding *Black Robe*. We are now getting into the serious stuff which will be largely beyond your comprehension, but I urge you to take a peripheral interest.

This co-production business seems to be like inventing the wheel – no-one really has a clue how to get it working, and so there is lots of information and misinformation that, at a later date, turns into information again. Still, it's all looking pretty positive and *if* they can hook a *bankable name*, I think we will be able to get it together quite well.

We are about to mix and deliver *The Saint*. Peter Best is doing the music. Apparently he did the music for *Barry McKenzie*. How can anyone be so old?!

Love to all,
Sue

FAX FROM Bruce to Sue, 20 November 1989
London

I'm in London working like mad preparing *Mister Johnson*. I was in Nigeria for a week looking at locations.

My agent and lawyer are still screaming over this film. They seem to think it won't happen, though I'll be surprised if they're right. Such a lot of money has already been spent. Shades of *Total Recall* – though I think we didn't make that one, did we?

Driving Miss Daisy is released in three cities in December. I'm keeping my fingers crossed. *I* think it's a good film.

Virginia and Trilby are still here and then joining me in Nigeria. I don't know how long they'll last there. It really is a tenth-world country. Benjamin is also coming out there to work.

I don't know yet who we're getting to play Laforgue in *Black Robe*. I spoke to William Hurt's agent, who said he's doing a play and not reading anything for months. He'll read it in February. Similarly with John Malkovich. Tom Berenger turned it down. Rutger Hauer and Sam Neill would both be fine for the role, but it seems they're not considered big enough stars! I tried to arrange a meeting with Nick Nolte (not that I'm at all convinced he's right) but his agent dodged me for weeks, right up until I left and came here to London.

I'll be pretty well uncontactable when I go to Nigeria, as they have no phones and no faxes. The post takes forever. A naked runner will bring me messages.

FAX FROM Sue to Bruce, 18 January 1990

This is a cheerio call before I depart for the US next Tuesday. Helen Watts is installed in the Film Finances executive suite for one year and I am almost a free person.

On the *Black Robe* front, there is nothing to report since I wrote last. We have moved the process forward as far as we can here, and we are still waiting for Telefilm Canada to contact the Australian Film Commission [the bodies responsible for regulating co-productions] to say they have approved it at their end. *Then* we can apply to the Film Finance Corporation for some of the Australian end money, and ask them to guarantee a further million or so which we will have to raise on the open market. It will be useful to meet the Canadians, and will make the rest of the process (assuming it goes ahead) a good deal easier. I understand they were making an offer to John Malkovich.

John Morris has been appointed chief executive of the Film Finance Corporation, the incumbent having resigned. It's far from good news for me, as John will never be fond of me after my review of SAFC [the South Australian Film Corporation]. He was most recently head of the much-weakened NSW Film Corporation, after Paul Riomfalvy was spring-cleaned by the Liberal Government.

I saw Barry Humphries the other day, and was introduced to Lizzie Spender. I was lunching at a new and super-trendy restaurant called Rockpool – all 1950s décor, hideously uncomfortable chairs and weird combinations of food in little dollops on big white plates. Barry and Lizzie stumbled in at about 2.30 and, after earnest discussions with the waiter, changed tables three times. Then Barry immediately got up clutching that chaotic Filofax and headed for the telephone. Lizzie seemed very fond of him, watching him concernedly and giving him a reassuring pat on the bum. He lied transparently that he had planned to call me, said he had lost my address so hadn't sent me a Christmas card, wrote the address on the back of a crumpled sheet of loose paper and promised me my earliest Christmas card for 1990.*

I have just been to see a film called *The Cook, The Thief, His Wife and Her Lover* by Peter Greenaway. It came to the Film Censorship Board of Review by way of an appeal against an R certificate. It is the most disgusting and phoney film I have ever seen. An incredibly irritating performance by Michael Gambon, and plot and dialogue concerned obsessively with the excretory organs. Graphic and gratuitous violence, gluttony – the lot. An absolute shocker.

---

* In 1986 I had produced *Les Patterson Saves the World* for Barry and his then wife Diane Milstead. SM

Did you have a nice Christmas in Nigeria? We might test out the postal system from Aspen to Jos, and see if we can get a snow-covered postcard through to brighten your life.

FAX FROM Bruce to Sue, 20 February 1990
Hill Station Hotel, Jos, Nigeria

Thanks for the various letters and information. I'm jealous of the skiing holiday – your card arrived today.

I had a telex from Michael Nolin asking me to okay an offer to Richard Gere for *Black Robe* but I think he's wrong for it. It's a difficult film to cast. My first choice was Daniel Day-Lewis though Alliance hadn't heard of him. Might be a different story now. They were to approach John Malkovich, so I assume he turned it down. Without the right actor it would be better not to do the film.

We're over halfway through *Mister Johnson* though I can't tell what it's going to be like. Odd, for sure.

T and V are both well. They seem to like it here.

LETTER FROM Sue to Bruce, 23 February 1990

I saw *Driving Miss Daisy* in Los Angeles, well before the nominations were announced and I really loved it. Congratulations on all the Academy Award nominations – the most of any picture. Wow! But *how* can a film get all those acknowledgements and no nomination for the director? It's completely crazy. It's a much better film than *Dead Poets Society* and infinitely better directed than *Born on the Fourth of July*, which made me feel slightly ill for more reasons than the enema closeups. Maybe you have to go in for 'A Bruce Beresford Film' if that's what it takes.*

---

* The Directors' Guild of America requires that directors take the possessive credit on all films. Bruce disliked this and refused to have it on his films. SM

I had a pleasant day in Toronto with Alliance. Robert Lantos was not there unfortunately, he was in Monte Carlo but I couldn't wait for his return. We took a couple of meetings and tossed a few scenarios around. Alliance is pondering the best structure for the film and this is being heavily influenced by your wishes about casting.

They have an offer for foreign [rights] from Carolco and an offer for the US from MGM. The MGM offer is conditional upon the 'big' name – hence the message about Richard Gere, who is MGM-approved. (*What* a strange business we're in!) I told them your response about Richard Gere but I guess they were hoping you'd like the idea – because that would have made it easy for them.

The alternative is to drop MGM and go with the foreign deal and a 'smaller' actor. This would mean a lower budget (reduced largely by cutting the shooting schedule). This would mean it could be offered to Daniel Day-Lewis or Sam Neill. This scenario appeals to me partly because it will be easier for me to structure the Australian money in a way that will please the investors. Without boring you too much, the MGM/Caralco deal would tie up the whole world, leaving only Australia for the Australian investors to recoup from, and even Rita [the dog] could figure out what that means. If the US was not presold, we could hold it out as a carrot for the Australian investors. Finally, I have a feeling that the film might just be a hell of a lot better made on this scale than on the full-blown, Hollywood-job situation.

At this moment Robert Lantos is considering what to do. Presumably if it's to be Plan B, he will approach Daniel Day-Lewis (who will cost them a heck of a lot more now than when you first suggested him). I will know early next week and then be able to start moving on financing the Australian end.

I believe you are now going back to the UK for post-production. I guess you will be able to see a lot of Adam and Cordelia. I had three days in LA, rang your house in case Virginia was there. A lady with a heavy accent told me you were both 'in Africa for one year'. Perhaps she needs to be rebriefed.

We are in the throes of yet another federal election, the two eminent choices being Hawke and Peacock. I have almost entirely stopped listening to the radio and reading the newspapers.

LETTER FROM Sue to Bruce, 18 March 1990

Bill Shanahan called me to say Sam Neill has read *Black Robe* and would like to talk to you about the role. I have heard nothing more about Daniel Day-Lewis.

Driving Miss Daisy has opened here and everyone is talking about it. I'm attaching Evan Williams' review – he can find *almost* nothing to criticise!

I am going to The Academy Awards at the Opera House. The bash is between 11 and 3, and you have to wear evening dress, as they are doing some kind of live cross to the Awards. Pretty silly. Tickets are exclusively reserved for distributors and their hangers-on, but Helen [Watts] got a couple as Bryan Brown and Rachel Ward are presenting. We will be standing by to boo whoever gets Best Director.*

Business is fairly quiet here at the moment. The collapse of the television networks has knocked the production staple of the last few years – the mini series.

---

* *Driving Miss Daisy* won Best Picture. I heard people in the ladies' loo congratulating the Australian publicist as if she had personally made the film. SM

31/3/90

Dear Sue,

The main idea of this is to test my new fax, which in true British style, is made as complex & expensive as possible.

I spoke to Lantos yesterday. He says that Day-Lewis isn't interested in the role, & as I said to you, trying to talk him into it is a total waste of time. Thinking more about the casting I'm tilting towards Timothy Dalton. Don't scream – he was absurdly miscast as James Bond, for which he lacks the lightness & flair; but I can see him as our tormented Priest.

BRANAGH

We're hanging around here until I see the rough cut of "Mr Johnson" next week. I'm very anxious. What have I made this time?

Saw "Cinema Paradiso" & am surprised it won the AA "Best Foreign Film". It has charm, but is over-full of comic villagers; [redacted] is weakly plotted & has a central theme of the hero's unrequited love that just seems ridiculous.

Dino is getting married next saturday. Martha is pregnant again, too!! He wants V & I to go over for it, but I don't think we can.

Phone & FAX NO is 351 0209

Love, Bruce

FAX FROM Sue to Bruce, 2 April 1990

Funnily enough I immediately saw the point of Timothy Dalton – he still has a reputation as a Shakespearean actor and thus 'serious', and he certainly looks right. In fact a part like Laforgue might considerably enhance his reputation. Thus he might go for it.

I spoke to Robert Lantos on Saturday. I found him rather crabby. I put the phone down feeling vaguely guilty; as if I'd been ticked off by the headmistress. No idea what for – I think I've done a pretty good job to date. Every indication from the FFC is that they are enthusiastic about being involved, which can only have been enhanced by *DMD*'s success.

FAX FROM Bruce to Sue, 9 April 1990

I've had a few talks with the mob at Alliance and, as far as I can tell, progress is being made on *Black Robe*.

I met Timothy Dalton who is very enthusiastic – *but* it seems there might be a Bond film beginning in September, in which case he's tied up. He won't even know for about a month. I think I should talk to Sam Neill as soon as possible. I'm having trouble thinking of other actors for the role – though I guess anything is hard to cast. Can you get me Sam's phone number?

Brian Moore is over here next week for the launch of his new book, so I'll be able to do some script revisions with him. I've been doing some background reading on the period and have come up with a few ideas.

FAX FROM Bruce to Robert Lantos, Stéphane Reichel, Michael Nolin, cc Sue, 11 April 1990

I had a meeting with Sam Neill which went very well. His agent called me to ask about an offer. I also had a call from Timothy Dalton's agent to say that the Bond film is *not* going ahead and that Timothy *is* available for us! This was a surprise as Robert told me the Bond definitely *was* going ahead. Can you find out the true story? It looks as if we're in a situation where we choose between the two actors. I think both are talented, but I lean a little towards Dalton.

FAX FROM Sue to Bruce, 12 April 1990

Interesting news about Sam and Timothy Dalton. Dalton is a slightly bigger name. I'll probably be a little sad if Sam doesn't get it, which means I'm probably too nice to be a producer!

Attached are a few clippings, including a piece on Dino in *Time*. I was especially amused by Stephen Greenwald, who went along with Dino hook, line and sinker till the going got rough.

Will you be cutting *Mister Johnson* till June? I would like to get you out here for a few days to charm the FFC.

Tom and I just went to Ayers Rock for the weekend – what a magnificent place. Uluru and the Olgas – so extraordinary, so mystical. Not even busloads of Scandinavian backpackers can impinge on their dignity and mystery.

Extract from *Time*, 'Star of His Own Dubious Epic', 9 April 1990

'Dino was clearly, unequivocably, unquestionably responsible for what happened to this company,' says Stephen Greenwald, DEG's former chairman. 'His attempts to evade that responsibility are reprehensible and ludicrous.' Greenwald says that De Laurentiis refused to resign unless he received a package of deals worth $110 million. He soon settled for $280,000.

FAX FROM Bruce to Sue, 1 May 1990

The meeting with Lantos was fine. I gather the deal is done with Jake Eberts [Canadian financier] but they're anxious about the Aussie end. Tim Dalton and his agent are buggering around because of the Bond film and I've suggested we go for a definite yes or no by Friday or put in an offer to Sam Neill. We could lose both of them with procrastination.*

I think I'll have to be in Canada in early June and fly back here weekends for the mix!

FAX FROM Sue to Bruce, 9 May 1990

You and Virginia might enjoy the attached bit of Sydney society nonsense, 'The Making of an Australian Princess'. The groom ran away with the best man a couple of days before the wedding in Venice, and no-one can figure out why there was a wedding in the first place. The bride has since had her interview on *60 Minutes*, remarkable only for her statement that her sexual relationship with the prince was excellent (*that* was news, the *SMH* remarked the next morning). We are still awaiting the prince's side of the story.

With luck we should have our official co-production status for *Black Robe* within a few days. Phillip Adams [chair of the AFC] and someone from Telefilm are to sign the agreement in Cannes this weekend. We have delivered all the material to the FFC and are now waiting for them to get their act together, call a board meeting and decide whether to give us $5 million. It will take about a week to get all the board members together.

Still no news on Timothy [Dalton] versus Sam [Neill].

---

* Both Sam Neill and Timothy Dalton turned out to be actors not admired by the Canadian investor, Jake Eberts. Finance people often call the tune on casting and are renowned for their lack of knowledge. BB

FAX FROM Sue to Bruce, 22 May 1990

Just to let you know this morning the board of the FFC deferred a decision on *Black Robe* till 31 May. It seems like they were in a dirty mood; I think they are keen to show who's in charge – the bureaucrats of course, not the filmmakers.

I am *extremely* pissed off. But I don't intend to lose the war.

Did you ever know Brian White? One of the best radio journalists there ever was, and a very nice bloke. He died this morning of a stroke, aged 56.

On a lighter note, Tony Ginnane was placed in receivership.*

FAX FROM Sue to Bruce, 5 June 1990

After our talk Alison Barrett called back and said yes, she could do the [Australian] casting, and would very much like to. That's what she's like – always comes through in the end! And as it happens she has just been casting nineteen-year-old boys for some other flick, so she was up to speed on who's around.

She has given it some thought and come up with three names. She reckons these are the only ones who have the level of ability to carry such a big role, and the appropriate looks. For instance, she mentioned Noah Taylor – he is a fine young actor – but he's so thin and frail he wouldn't look right and might have difficulty coping physically with the role.

Simon Kaye. She says he's a nice looking boy. I don't know him.

Russell Crowe. Russell is a little older than nineteen, but very talented. He's good-looking and quite physical (but not in the Aussie soap-star way you wanted to avoid). Alison says he has Mel Gibson's voice.

---

* Antony I. Ginnane – producer of films such as *Patrick*, *Fantasm Comes Again* and *The Survivor* – was never down for long. SM

One way or another, Russell is going to go places.

Aden Young. He is in fact half Canadian, and has been trying to acquire an Aussie accent. He is quite young and not hugely experienced, but Alison feels he is very interesting.

We are going to put them on tape on Thursday evening.

Still plodding on with the FFC. Making slow and tortuous progress.

FAX FROM Bruce to Sue, 6 June 1990
Subject: Assorted ratbags

Do you want me to write a letter to the board re the film? I saw Jake's letter and it seems to say everything succinctly.

I'm going to LA on Monday mainly to work with Brian Moore on the script. I'll be at my house. I don't think Noah Taylor is right – too gangly. I think we'll be using Lothaire Bluteau as Laforgue. He has the lead in *Jesus of Montreal.*

FAX FROM Sue to Bruce, 8 June 1990

We have taped the three young actors and the tape will go off over the weekend to your LA house.

If you feel disposed, a letter from you to Kim Williams [chair of the FFC] might not be a bad thing. Issues to be addressed are your enthusiasm for the film, its commercial potential and your desire to come back to Australia to finish it. It might be a good idea to run it by Robert Lantos. We are all putting our heads together to try and convince the buggers.

I went to an event at AFTRS [Australian Film, Television & Radio School] to do with newsreels, and all the old codgers were there – Ken Hall, Alex Ezzard, Ross King. An old devil called Hughie McInnes said to John Morris in front of several people, 'Jeez John, when you started at the Commonwealth Film Unit you were such an *insecure* boy.' Everyone laughed nervously and looked the other way.

Tomorrow is the start of the ski season. No snow of course. I have new skis and boots, which I am very anxious to try out. Will have to fit in between trips to Canada.

FAX FROM Sue to Bruce, 28 June 1990

The production manager called me this morning to say you will be somewhere else (London presumably?) from 4–15 July. This throws our plans for Aden into chaos. I was going to send him over next week. They mentioned some crazy plan to send him to London, which I don't agree with. The poor little bastard can't believe he's going to Canada – he came out to Australia for a holiday with his mother when he was nine, after his father died, and while they were here she decided to stay for good, so Aden never got to say goodbye to his friends. I would hate to have to tell him he's not going there after all.

I have just seen *Total Recall*. As you said, an eerie experience. They did a terrific job, and the special effects are incredible. It's a very good film. But it's a bit like seeing a part of your own life unravel – or were all those months in the showground just a dream?

FAX FROM Bruce to Sue, 28 June 1990

I agree that bringing Aden to Canada around 17–18 July would be best. I'm just leaving for Montreal now. Meeting first in Toronto with Lantos and a *very* odd casting lady.

Saw a good Dutch film – *The Vanishing*. Has the most horrific ending ever.

FAX FROM Sue to Bruce, 27 July 1990
PERSONAL

I went to the opening of *Blood Oath* the other night. The film is good, and Bryan Brown gives a great performance.

A highlight of the evening was the attendance at the screening of our favourite ex-wife... She was dressed in knee-length gold boots, a flared black leather mini skirt (I mean *mini*) topped by a black leather jacket with messages spelt out on it in large silver studs. Her 'date' (her word) was a 40-year-old female who was dressed in an equally short mini dress of hot pink taffeta. The film is about the degradation of the human spirit, brutal torture at the hands of an alien culture and the manipulation of justice for the ends of the powerful. After the movie everyone was soberly discussing the issues etc., etc., and the two of them standing around in their bizarre outfits looked like a couple of drag queens who had inadvertently crashed a meeting of the Masons.

The FFC approved investment in Black Robe in July 1990, completing the financing. Correspondence ceased while we were in production in Canada and post-production in Sydney.

FAX FROM Bruce to Jake Eberts, Majestic Films, 4 July 1991

In my view, for what it's worth, we're making a mistake in not showing this film [*Black Robe*] to the Venice Festival selection committee. The film has no star 'names' and is like no other film. It seems to me we need the kind of attention that a film festival could offer us. Some of my films of the past, notably *Breaker Morant* would have had no release whatever if it weren't for festival (notably Cannes) screenings and subsequent media attention.

Are you afraid to show the film to the Venice Committee because you have no faith in it and are afraid of rejection? This, of course, is always a possibility. But we would be no worse off – it certainly won't be shown if we don't submit it.

I am proud of the film and of everyone associated with its production. I regard it as my best film, no matter what its faults, and I'm pretty amazed that a prestige venue like the Venice Film Festival is considered worthless.

Having made the film there is no point hiding it, or disowning it. A few years ago a film of mine was invited to the Chicago Film Festival. The American distributor refused to put it in because an influential local critic 'may not like it' and his reports would be circulated all over America. I objected to this craven argument, but the film wasn't shown. About six months later when the film was released in Chicago the same critic (Roger Ebert) raved over it. If he'd been able to rave over it when it was in the festival we'd have had much more publicity out of it.

Regards,
Bruce Beresford

FAX FROM Bruce to Robert Lantos, cc Sue Milliken, 8 July 1991

I heard from the post-production supervisor that Goldwyn might want the throat cut removed from *Black Robe*. As you'd expect I'm hardly in favour of this mainly because the film is an honest one and this incident is part, an integral part, of the story and is in no way classifiable as gratuitous violence in the style of so many 1990s movies. Secondly, if the incident is removed or even re-cut, the scene will not be comprehensible. Thirdly, there is nowhere near as much violence in *Black Robe* as there is in *Dances with Wolves* or of a number of other respected, if violent, films.

The actual tortures of the Iroquois are already softened from the novel and I'm not anxious to take any punch out of the film. These guys circa 1634 were not a bunch of wusses. Times were tough.

The Indians were tough. The settlers were tough. We should go for it.

Regards,
Bruce

FAX FROM Sue to Bruce, 15 July 1991

Got your faxes and herewith what I have done re the trailer. I looked at the changes this morning – they're all pretty good. Only problem is they will probably send Alliance into a blue funk and may cause them to cancel the trailer altogether! They will *never* be able to make a decision off a bit of paper. I suppose I should have said 'no more changes' on Thursday, but I'm always keen to consider a better idea.

Tonight I will listen to the voiceover tapes. I know Tim Elliott's voice. He's pretty good, and he's available. So we'll probably go with him. Will let him listen to Frank [Wilson]. It needs a bit more punch though, I think. But I agree about the reading.

Also herewith a letter from our lawyer, Paula [Paizes], which says nice things well about the film. She pulled off a great coup the other day getting Hoyts to sign the distribution contract while we were in the boardroom. It was very cool.

Spoke to Lloyd Hart about Tom Haydon.* Seems there might be some money back from *The Last Tasmanian*, and outstanding debts are only about $5000. The only person I can think to ring who might be helpful with more money is Kim Williams – although I'm sure he has already given generously, as you have. I told Lloyd I'm good for a grand, and you might do two.

---

* Documentary filmmaker Tom Haydon died of cancer in his early fifties, leaving debts. A fund was set up to help his family.

FAX FROM Bruce to Tom Rothman, Samuel Goldwyn Company, 18 July 1991

Dear Tom

Obviously I don't want to be unreasonable about the throat-cutting scene and I suppose it would be possible to restructure it so there is more of the closeup of the Indian actually doing the cutting and less of the child. I've seen the TV version and I don't think it is really entirely clear what has happened and that certainly weakens the impact of the scene. I directed the scene in such a way that the violence comes as a surprise. This means that until it actually happens there isn't much to see and that means that attempts to restructure result in obscurity. Still, if we *had* to change it we could try.

The odd thing about all this is that I've been worried critics would attack us (me) for *softening* the impact of the novel, in which they not only kill the child but chop it up and eat it!

Anyway as I said, the shot probably can be changed. It might be a mistake and detrimental to the film.

Regards,
Bruce

FAX FROM Sue to Bruce, 19 July 1991

The trailer is mixed and on its way to you. It works very well. The Delerue drums work very well over the action. How *could* those Canadians have thought they could improve on it?

I've finalised the letter to Tom Haydon's friends. Kim was actually quite nice on the last phone call. It should only take a week to get it out.

FAX FROM Bruce to Sue, 30 July 1991

Georges Delerue

Most film scores are quite dreadful – thumping and banging away relentlessly and frequently being used only to cover up the errors of the director and/or to supply the emotions that the actors failed to convey. Most of the composers do not do their own orchestrations (though the orchestrators are rarely credited), which means the music lacks a personal style, and the main melodies are frequently unashamedly lifted from classical works.

Delerue though, orchestrates all of his music himself and has a remarkable gift for melody.

The range of his work is astonishing, from the romantic lyricism of *Jules and Jim* to the cabaret music of *The Conformist* and the medieval drama of *Black Robe*. In common with all first-rate composers, Delerue's signature, the touch that identifies a score as being his, rather than an anonymous piece, is always apparent after a few bars – it is not just the lyricism, or the polished orchestration, but the spirit of the man himself.

FAX FROM Sue to Bruce, 5 August 1991

Hugh McGowan [head of Hoyts distribution] was on the phone today haemorrhaging over *The Australian* interview – 'Gloomiest film ever made.' He wondered if in future interviews you could say it's the best thing you've ever done instead?

FAX FROM Bruce to Robert Lantos, cc Sue Milliken, 23 August 1991

As I've said before, I think it's a mistake for the Goldwyn Company to want to change the throat-cutting shot but I understand the difficult position you are in regarding the sale.

On the other hand, I can't see why Goldwyn should care if (a) the shot is included in countries like Australia where there is no objection to it, and (b) why are they interested in concealing the fact they changed the shot? If they feel strongly that it's in bad taste or whatever reason they have for wanting it changed then they shouldn't have any qualms about saying so. In any case, quite a lot of press people have already seen the film with the shot included, so it's likely to be commented on anyway.

Does Goldwyn actually have the legal right to insist that the film conforms to his version in all territories? Why don't we just show the original version wherever the local distributor wants it?

FAX FROM Robert Lantos to Sue Milliken, cc Bruce Beresford and Jake Eberts, 23 August 1991

The debate to preserve 'the throat-cutting shot' took place between Sam Goldwyn and Guy East on one side and myself on the other. It resulted in Goldwyn making it a deal breaker, declaring that 'The Goldwyn Company was the wrong distributor for the film if this shot was in it.' They believe that with the shot left in, the film would not qualify for an R rating, which would make it practically unmarketable in the US.

At that point, after talking to Bruce we backed off, but tried to hold out for the festival screening. However, Goldwyn's position was that making a change after a public screening (where critics will see the film) would result in an uncalled-for controversy. This was argued until it, too, became a deal breaker. Finally, we reluctantly agreed to make the change.

I cannot see the value of raising this again now. There is nothing we can do without jeopardising the release of the film. It is like pouring acid on a wound.

FAX FROM Robert Lantos to Bruce, cc Sue Milliken and Jake Eberts, 26 August 1991

Goldwyn's main argument about the shot had to do with their judgment that, if left in, the film would fail to get an R rating and we have a contractual obligation to deliver an R rating. Also, if the press attention focuses on this issue it would be detrimental to the film's performance and that hurts all of us.

On the other hand, there is no reason why the film could not play with the 'shot' included in Australia or any other country which so wishes.

Finally, we are dealing here with a few frames of film. I do not propose to be cavalier about the importance of the shot in question. However, in the context of the monumental effort expended to make this film and the superb results, let us put this behind us.

FAX FROM Sue to Bruce, 26 August 1991 *Rich in Love* Production Office

Thanks for the copy of your fax to Robert Lantos. I thought it was worth stirring the whole thing up one more time – and of course it is utterly absurd to screen the censored version at the festival [Toronto, world premiere]. Especially as so many people have seen the original version.

Norman [Banks], my contact at the FFC, called this morning with a little news of Clayton and Ken.* It seems that they met with no

---

* Bruce had seen an article about the development of a film on the Australian cycling champion and politician, Hubert Opperman. The script, *A Chance for Glory*, was written by Peter Yeldham. Bruce liked the idea and we set about contacting a Melbourne duo, Ken Lyons and Clayton Sinclair who owned the script, with the offer to come on board as producer and director. At first they seemed enthusiastic, but as time went on they became more and more elusive. SM

interest in the project in England or France, but an American studio – Norman did not know which – had taken it up and told them not to bother with any Australian connection, that they have thrown out the Peter Yeldham script and plan to rewrite it and put an American director on it. Norman seems to think that this would have come about because Clayton and Ken may have told them they have $100m to finance films, including this one. It may not even be a real studio – it could be an agent or who knows what. Norman thought they were foolish and that it was a great shame as it won't come to anything. However they probably now believe they can be rich and famous, as everyone seems to be after the script.

I think that time will take care of them. Sooner or later their cashflow must run out. At some point there could well be a chance to pick it up out of the wreckage.

FAX FROM Bruce to Sue, 27 August 1991
Charleston, Virginia

I've just spoken to Sam Goldwyn who said he's very thrilled to have *Black Robe* and has just had a very successful test screening. It seems that the Canadians are no more efficient with him than they are with us, so please send them copies of all our publicity material and Belinda's poster.

FAX FROM Bruce to Sue, 31 August 1991

Belinda's poster just arrived and I think it's very good. The single image is arresting and stylish. Virginia said 'Oh it's just a picture of a priest, who'll want to see that?' BUT it is selling the film we've made and I believe that's important.

I also think the catchphrase is effective – ironic.

See you on Thursday in Toronto. Smart thinking of you to keep chasing them up about the cinema and projection. Is the print they're showing one done in a Canadian lab? If so, we could be in trouble. Should we ship over an Australian print as a backup?

Will you bring a big jar of Vegemite?

Also, there's a new book out on Jeffrey Smart. If you have time could you get it for me as I want it as a present for someone.

FAX FROM Sue to Bruce, 2 September 1991

Good news you will be in Toronto.

A year's supply of Vegemite is being arranged.

I can't ship the print from here because ours have the offending shot in them. However Gordon made some prints off the negative, so it *should* be okay.

FAX FROM Sue to Bruce and Virginia, 18 September 1991

You asked for art books – so I'm sending you several! They seem to cover a reasonably wide range of Australian painting of the period you wanted.

I had a couple of pretty unscintillating days in Toronto after you left. I went down to Sue Murdoch's [production manager on *Black Robe*] for lunch and a ride on one of her extremely tall horses. The weather was perfect and the farm is very beautiful in that ordered, English/Ontario way. Monday I went into Alliance and Gordon gave me a tape of their trailer – it's heavily based on yours, but has a *very* heavy-handed and lugubrious soundtrack, and a narrator who sounds as though he's competing for the Tennessee Ernie Ford Award.

I saw *Dead Again* while killing time in Toronto. I'm told that Dame Edna's question to Kenneth Branagh should she ever get him on her show will be: 'How do you explain your extraordinary humility?'

Barry has a crush on the Film Finances chief, Richard Soames and his wife Dodie. They met a few weeks ago in LA and Barry calls up all the time, wanting to see them and have meals with them. Barry and Lizzie have lunched at his house in Malibu a couple of times. Richard and I think it's because Barry is a bit anonymous in LA and being the quintessential pom with a heavy Australian connection, at least Richard knows who he is.

I saw the Goldwyn people in LA, they were very polite and showed me their poster concept. They say they are going to keep away from the religious aspect, like Roadshow tried to keep away from the Aboriginal aspect in *The Fringe Dwellers.*

I saw Hoyts this morning. They have the trailer running in 80 cinemas and it will be in 200 by Christmas. I hope everyone is not sick to death of it by February.

My pal at the FFC who knew Ken Lyons got the chop a couple of weeks ago. Apparently John Morris flew into town and fired him and the other investment executive in the Melbourne office. I thought Norman was doing quite a good job. I will try and meet that accountant, David Butterfield, when I'm in Melbourne, so as to keep tabs on Clayton and Ken.

The recession deepens and Kerry Packer, according to *Four Corners*, only pays 10 cents in the dollar tax.

FAX FROM Bruce to Sue, 24 September 1991
Rich in Love Production Office, Charleston SC

I guess you saw the good reviews for *Black Robe*. I had a call from Goldwyn's office a few days ago to do a brief, very brief, interview with the *LA Times Magazine*. Evidently they are the *only* people so far who've agreed to write anything about the film. I think it's the old problem of 'lack of stars'. We had the same difficulty with *Driving Miss Daisy*. No-one wanted to know about it. It's astonishing. If I was doing a film with Goldie Hawn we would effortlessly get vast magazine and newspaper coverage, plus she'd be on all the chat shows being as inane as ever.

Cordelia is here and has been with the camera department but I think the job is too complex for her.* Sometimes I think very intelligent people are at a disadvantage because they ask too many questions and are buried under detail. Luckily, you and I don't have this problem.

Barry has called me a few times from LA. His TV show is being well publicised here and could establish him – I know he fervently hopes so.

Clive James has a new TV show in London and a new novel out in a month.

FAX FROM Sue to Bruce, 27 September 1991

I've just been in to Hoyts and approved the final artwork for Belinda's poster. Hugh [McGowan] is excited because he says he is getting a girl who he thinks is the only publicist in Australia with a brain to come and work on all his pictures from November. Good for us.

Alliance sent Hoyts 49 copies of the Australian trailer the other day. Nobody asked for them, and of course Hoyts have made all the copies they want. Alliance are a *truly* remarkable outfit.

How about that Dun & Bradstreet report on Lyons and Sinclair? Who organised that? It doesn't tell much, *except* that they kicked off with $500,000 – no wonder they are having such a good time! I'd kill to know where the cash came from. Seems unbelievable.

FAX FROM Bruce to Sue, 29 September 1991

The books arrived a few days ago. They're all fine and will come in handy.

We've just finished two weeks filming. The cast seems to be very good. Albert Finney is an incredibly accomplished actor. Like Morgan Freeman, he has terrific technical knowledge and does

---

* Cordelia is now an award-winning cinematographer.

everything he can to make the shots work as planned. He is also very good natured and free of the snobbery which seems to strike so many successful actors.

Shay Martin faxed me about 'great news' on the Chow Hayes story. How this could possibly be true with no script I can't imagine. The book about Chow Hayes is fascinating but there is a lot of work shaping it for a film. For a start, Hayes is an utterly remorseless killer who quite frankly admits wiping out scores of opponents without ever giving any of them the slightest chance. At one point he puts five bullets into a man he thinks *might* be planning to kill him, then ingratiates himself with the bloke's wife and convinces her he is wrongly suspected and persuades her she should provide him with an alibi.

Barry tells me NBC *is* picking up his pilot for a series. He's very pleased about it.

FAX FROM Sue to Bruce, 4 October 1991

I'm faxing a copy of the release schedule for the film, which Majestic sent. They've been very good, sent me stuff as soon as I asked for it.

The AFI Awards were last night. John Duigan got the Byron Kennedy Award – $10,000. It was announced by Gough Whitlam but there was no-one there to accept on John's behalf, and no recorded message from him, so after looking around a bit bemused, Gough sort of wandered off the stage, award in one hand. Peter Weir was a presenter and Fred Schepisi got the Raymond Longford Award. So much for our efforts to get it for Lee [Robinson]. It's about time they recognised some of the lower profile people such as Arthur Cambridge. As usual the night was a bit Gulargambone RSL but some of it was okay. Frankie J. Holden compèred. A fabulous Aboriginal rock band called Yothu Yindi opened the show – one of those Yunupingus from Arnhem Land is the lead singer. He's in black jeans and shirt, and the others are in feathers and ochre, with headset microphones. There is a didgeridoo player and a white guitarist. The sound is fantastic. *Proof* took out best film.

I saw David Stratton at the party and thanked him for his review of *Black Robe*. He said he absolutely adores the film. He said he was *furious* with Hoyts for not inviting him to a screening (meaning the one you came to when all the press were there). He got in quite a tizz at the thought. I was a bit sorry I'd brought it up. The party was at the back of the Opera House, overlooking the harbour. But about midnight one of those insufferable rock bands shook the place and we headed for home.

I think I'd give Chow Hayes a miss by the sound of things. Your description of the character is a total turn-off.

Nothing new on Lyons and Sinclair.

Anne Whitehead [scriptwriter] just called me to say the Queensland Film Corporation deferred a decision to fund a third draft of the Paraguay script until she provides a contract between her and me as producer. Bloody bureaucrats! So now we have to go through this farce to satisfy them. However she says she is already halfway through the draft. She has had to take another job, pending getting the money, but will probably finish the draft by the end of the year.

The colour stills for *Black Robe* which I selected in Toronto arrived the other day, and Hoyts were really pleased with them – thought they were much better than most of the Alliance selection. Alliance must have had the janitor select them.

I guess Barry is going to be mega-famous at last, once his series goes out on NBC.

FAX FROM Bruce to Sue, 13 October 1991

We've finished four weeks on *Rich in Love* and it's going okay though very hard to tell what it will be like.

I had a bizarre phone call from someone who works with Shay Martin. She repeated that they have $12 million for *Chow Hayes* and was (is) in Los Angeles where she'd offered the lead role and producer (!!!!!!!!!!!!!!!!!!!!!!!!) to Kirk Douglas. I told her that (a) without a script any moves of this kind were premature (b) Kirk Douglas is not a producer (c) he is also no longer an actor (d) he is far too old to play Chow Hayes (e) Chow was an Australian gunman. How would someone like Douglas be explained?

Give *Rosencrantz and Guildenstern Are Dead* a wide berth, despite its Venice Grand Prix. Just like the play it's an affected piece of claptrap.

Barry tells me NBC are doing another special very soon.

Had a nice letter from Pat Lovell [producer] who had seen *Black Robe* in Sydney. What's she doing these days?

FAX FROM Sue to Bruce, 16 October 1991

The earlier you can come to Sydney, the better.

Now that dear old Norman is no longer at FFC I need a new source for info on Clayton and Ken.

Shay Martin's assistant did mention something on the phone about Kirk Douglas but I immediately discarded the information as irrelevant. No-one ever tells you they have two million dollars for a picture, and whenever they tell you they have ten million or more, you know it's fantasy time. Not one of these incredible stories, has ever, in my experience, come to anything. But in our business, that doesn't stop 'em.

I'm glad Pat Lovell wrote to you. She really seemed to love the film. She's not doing too much – it's so hard to raise money these days, and I don't think she had much success with any of her projects. She has just moved her office from West Street back to her house at Clareville so I suspect times are tough.

Should we get Phillip Adams to see *Black Robe*? He's still quite influential with the general public – two columns a week in the *Australian*, plus his radio show. If he decides to push something, he really gives it a shove.

Today we seem to be having a heatwave, which is alarming, since it's only October. Maybe it will rain, which would be good for the park, but not so good for the seven pictures we (Film Finances) have shooting now. As usual they are all going in a bunch and there'll be nothing happening after Christmas.

I've just been to Masterpieces from the Guggenheim at the art gallery. Picasso, Braque, Miró, plus someone called Delaunay who did interesting things with the Eiffel Tower and coloured circles. Apparently the Guggenheim is being renovated, so we got 'em.

FAX FROM Sue to Bruce, 25 October 1991

I met with that accountant, David Butterfield, in Melbourne. The meeting more or less confirmed my telephone impression of him. *You* might like him because he used to be an opera singer before he was an accountant. He would not tell me anything about Clayton and Ken except that he thinks they are pretty clever. So it was more or less a waste of time. I subsequently asked someone else in Melbourne about them. His assessment of the pair (without any prompting) was almost word for word mine. His guess about what has happened to the script is that they have sold it to some small distributor who bought it because you were interested, and who will try and dish it up themselves – and nothing will ever come of it. Let's see.

FAX FROM Bruce to Sue, 28 October 1991

Enclosed is a copy of the first New York ad for *Black Robe*. As you can see, it's quite awful. I haven't said anything yet to Goldwyn. What's the point? I complained about the pathetic press handouts, but they obviously have no style at all. Dick Zanuck told me last night that

Goldwyn is notoriously cheap, and judging by the handouts and the lousy design of this press ad, he might be right.

The Sinclair Lyons saga is endless. No-one has been in touch with me about it. It's still very hard to work out why if they don't have any money they weren't willing to sell the script to us.

Filming is going okay, we're just starting nights.

FAX FROM Sue to Bruce, 30 October 1991

I think Tracey [Mair, publicist] will be good. She really seems to love the film – at first I thought she was possibly doing a PR job on the producer, but she kept up the enthusiasm for over an hour, so I concluded it was probably genuine.

Goldwyns showed me a rough of the artwork when I was in LA – although at that time they stressed it was not final. They were adamant they wanted to stay away from the religious theme (after all it's a film about a priest – why would you want to show that?). They certainly weren't going to listen to me.

The responses from the press screenings in New York were pretty good – I especially liked the one which *didn't* like it – said it went from 'slow to violent'!

I have a lot of pictures shooting now I am completion-guaranteeing. A couple of the directors are being quite difficult, and shooting ridiculous ratios (would it surprise you to learn that one of them is Bob Ellis?).

Aden dropped by yesterday, he's as gorgeous as ever.

FAX FROM Bruce to Sue, 4 November 1991

We're supposed to finish shooting here on 16 November. This means I could come to Sydney immediately after that.

The Australian poster is quite wonderful. I don't accept this criticism, from Lantos or Goldwyn, that featuring the priest is bad for business. There is no point disguising what the film is all about!

Why do distributors all too often want to sell some film other than the one they've made? Sam Goldwyn told me he wants to sell it as action/adventure but his ads don't do this at all. A shot of Indians in a canoe, all with stuck-on heads, makes it look like a mutants' picnic. He's wound up with neither action/adventure, nor the class and style of the Aussie ads.

Some of the critical comments here were amazingly ignorant on matters of fact. All their ideas of Indians come from movies showing them in the nineteenth century, and they were inaccurate more often than not. A few commented on the Indian girl being 'too beautiful'. Racist as well as ignorant. Virtually all the Jesuit *Relations* commented on the extreme physical beauty of the Indians.* Actually a major problem in making the film was in finding Indians who weren't overweight.

I think there is no point whatever in advertising this film as 'by the director of *Driving Miss Daisy*. I don't think this will get anyone into any cinema, no-one who saw *Daisy* will want to see *Black Robe*. The best quote is the one from the Toronto paper – 'barbaric, compelling, mesmeric'.

FAX FROM Bruce to Sue, 5 November 1991

I must say I am very fed up with Goldwyn and their amateur distribution agency. Firstly their press handout kit was a total disgrace, uninformed, misspelt, and seemingly aimed at a class of five-year-olds. The real blow, though, was their pathetic poster. I'm still reeling from that one. Only the Roadshow *Fringe Dwellers* poster was worse, though I suppose the Phillip Adams-approved design for the *Don's Party* poster would be racing them for the title 'worst design of all time'.

---

* *The Relations des Jésuites de la Nouvelle-France* are letters and reports written from Quebec in the seventeenth century to headquarters in France, and later published. Bruce used them as part of his research for *Black Robe*.

I gather from Lenny Hirshan [Bruce's agent] that the figures were good in New York for the first weekend and the audience reaction positive.

The only film I've done which had first class promotion and advertising all the way through was *Driving Miss Daisy*. It's far from being the best film I've done but just look at the result.

I also think the Canadian campaign on *Black Robe* is good – again with excellent results.

Don't tell me there is another Australian film being made called *Fortress*?! It's like having two directors called George Miller.

We are finished night shoots and back on days.

FAX FROM Bruce to Sue, 7 November 1991

I've talked with both Sam Goldwyn and Robert Lantos in the past couple of days and they're quite keen that I *don't* go to Sydney immediately after the shoot of *Rich in Love* as they would like me to help promote *Black Robe* in Los Angeles for a week and possibly go to the Canadian Awards. Would it make a lot of difference if I came to Sydney late in November and stayed till, say, the end of the first week of December? Wouldn't the media people Hugh wants still be around? Anyway, let me know what you think.

I suppose you know there have been a lot more *Black Robe* reviews. I'd say mostly favourable. The film seems to stir people up. I'm disappointed that Lothaire is generally not treated too well and I think it boils down to the problem of a central character who can't confide his fears and problems to anyone. In fact a man like him wouldn't have said anything even if people were around he could have talked to. Bluteau does give the role a strong sense of spirituality and belief. How many actors could have done that? It's as difficult as finding someone to convincingly paint a nativity scene. It doesn't happen any more because no-one has that kind of faith any more.

I like this Canadian ad. Quotes are good and the imagery is strong, though Canadian papers all look like they're printed through a sieve.

FAX FROM Sue to Bruce, 8 November 1991

It's funny about Lothaire – I think the problem might be that the character/performance is somehow less than the sum of its parts. It's all there – the motivation, the temptation, the struggle – the human relief after he's lost in the forest. The wonderful moment after 'Do you love us?'

I have always found the farewell between Laforgue and Daniel on the beach unsatisfying. They have been through so much together, and for Laforgue not even to bend a little and show some warmth to Daniel when he is seeing him for the last time seems to diminish Laforgue as a human being. So maybe this has an effect on others, too. Otherwise I'm sure you're right that it is the nature of that particular character in that particular time which handicaps his human responses.

Hollywood might have made Laforgue more accessible, but it would probably have cast Burt Reynolds in the role. I think the film is a lot better off as it is.

FAX FROM Bruce to Sue, 12 November 1991

It now looks as if we'll finish shooting on 18 November and I should be back in LA the following evening. If it turns out there isn't much I could do here in the US on *Black Robe* I'd like to know as I could go skiing for a few days. I'm a bit tired after this shoot and would like a few days relaxing.

I toyed with the idea of making more of the final farewell of Daniel and Laforgue, but decided that a show of emotion from Laforgue at this point wouldn't ring true. I thought he was going as far as he dared in telling Daniel to go off with the girl as she needed him more. In the situation, I don't think I'd have been wildly effusive over some bloke who'd cleared off and left me alone in the wilderness.

The scene I regret losing (not even filming) is the one where they met the two fur traders. This would've presented Laforgue with a last-minute opportunity to go back to Quebec, and safety – an offer he thought about and then turned down.*

FAX FROM Sue to Bruce, 13 November 1991

The piece in the *LA Times* is quite good. Your quote had me laughing, it was like hearing you say it. Approx. another 40 pages of press have just arrived from Alliance, so we cannot say the film is being ignored. I understand it is the highest grossing film in Canada still, and I am sure you know it opened well in LA. Michelle also sent me the offending poster. I think the problem of the funny-looking people was because they made a composite of several stills and it

---

* Against my wishes this scene was cut for budget reasons. BB

went through so many generations it all became distorted. Even if it had been just one still, it would have been a long way down the queue in a design competition.

I am in Perth right now.

FAX FROM Bruce to Sue, 17 November 1991

We finish shooting tomorrow. We're flying back to LA on 20 November. I assume the fax there is working (haven't been in the house for years). Virginia, Trilby and I can fly to Sydney on 27 November.

I guess you saw the wonderful *New Yorker* review of *Black Robe.* Also, today, the *New York Times* has written another review, in effect, far more favourable than the [Vincent] Canby one.

FAX FROM Sue to Bruce, 19 November 1991

I am catching up with the reviews gradually – there are hundreds of them! Most come across as if the writer is enjoying having something worthwhile to write about, for a change. Poor Lothaire still fares badly, with only the occasional positive notice. I continue to ponder on this; the only actor I can think of who might have done what the critics seem to want is Daniel Day-Lewis – meaning he could have played it the same way but his own personality might have given the character another dimension. I also wonder whether, in fact, the film would have provoked the positive intellectual reaction about the interplay between the two cultures *if* Laforgue had been a more accessible fellow. I think not. But it is intriguing – because under no circumstances could Lothaire's performance be called anything but dedicated and focussed.

I saw Suzanne Haydon the other night. (At a party at Film Australia, where we all had to wear funny hats.) I asked her about the tax bill and she said she has made some sales of Tom's films and was able to pay it herself, and that this was what she wanted. So I don't think there's too much more we can do.

I'm looking forward to seeing all three of you. It's real Sydney spring weather here now – cool, fresh mornings, blue skies and warm days. Perfect weather for lunch at Berowra Waters [Tony and Gay Bilson's fabled Berowra Waters Inn].

FAX FROM Sue to Bruce, 21 November 1991

Got your travel arrangements today. Be sure to let me know if you need anything done re the house (except for making the beds).

FAX FROM Bruce to Sue, 21 November 1991

Well we're back in the LA house. It's surprisingly well kept. Usually tenants break everything mechanical. It'd be nice if you or a slave could meet us but it isn't crucial. We can easily get a cab.

FAX FROM Bruce to Sue, 19 December 1991

I saw the rough cut of *Rich in Love*. It's overlong but substantially the movie. God knows if anyone will be interested.

I've heard from Majestic in London to say *Black Robe* is opening at the Plaza(?) in the West End for a 'minimum run of eight weeks'. Sounds like good news, especially after my four-day run on *Breaker Morant* and five days on *Mister Johnson*. I've urged them to use the Australian poster and not the byline 'From the director of *Driving Miss Daisy*', which I think is the kiss of death.

We saw Barry and Lizzie, both in cheerful mood because of the success of the TV special.

Cordelia is here at the moment and is going to France to join Rhoisin for Christmas. She is worried what kind of job she'll get. We're spending Christmas with Dino [De Laurentiis] and family.

He's trying to persuade me to join some other directors (Fellini, he claims) in doing the Bible for TV.

FAX FROM Sue to Bruce, 20 December 1991

Nothing too exciting happening here – apart from getting a new prime minister, as I'm sure you've heard. Keating will be a very different can of worms to Hawke. The vote was 51–56.

I had a meeting with Hoyts yesterday, then Hugh took Tracey and me to lunch at Tre Scalini. We looked again at the electronic press kit sent by Alliance. Surprisingly, it is extremely good, and we will use it here. Tracey told me that Lothaire is confirmed to come here for the last week in February. His agent told Tracey that rather than a holiday on the Barrier Reef when he's finished, he asked for *two* air tickets! *Who* could he possibly be bringing?*

I hope you got my fax thanking you for the cake. As happens every year I am already in trouble for doing a quality check. Tom likes to take it to the farm intact.

Tell Cordelia not to fall into the trap of brilliant people and spread herself too wide. Pretend to be a plodder like me and concentrate on one thing for a while. At least till she can earn some money at it! She shows good sense in resisting acting. Actors have no control over their own lives at all, unless they are part of the 1% who make it.

Christmas with Dino should be nice. Does he still have that great Italian cook? We are having it with our old friends Anne and John Fraser (I do the potatoes).

Happy Christmas to all and love from Sue, Tom and Rita.

---

* It turned out to be his mother.

CHAPTER TWO:1992

On-screen sparkle dulled by dim-witted judging

FAX FROM Sue to Bruce and Virginia, 10 January 1992

I hope you had a nice Christmas. Ours was great, the weather was pleasantly cool which assisted with the over-eating. We then went to the farm, planning to stay a week, but the cool weather turned into a deluge. After three days the creeks were running a banker and there was no sign of it stopping, so we threw everything into the car and came home. The rain hasn't stopped since. Soon, instead of the worst drought in living memory, people will be up to their dining room tables in muddy water.

My tickets arrived for skiing. Will you have room for me on my way through LA, or should I book a hotel?

FAX FROM Bruce to Sue, 12 January 1992
2111 N. Bronson, LA

You can stay here of course. Let us know your flight no. and we'll meet you.

Goldwyn has been doing virtually nothing for the Academy campaign. Maybe it isn't worthwhile because of the lack of Golden Globe nominations. (I was sure we'd get at least one!) But you never know with these things.

I'm editing away furiously and trying to rework the *Les Misérables* material into a script, though the French guys haven't sent much material yet. No word at all from Cameron Mackintosh [theatre producer].*

Any news of Ken and Clayton? Peter Yeldham sent me a copy of a letter to old Sir Hubert Opperman, but I've heard nothing further.

FAX FROM Sue to Bruce, 13 January 1992

I'm looking forward to seeing you both. On no account are you to meet me. The last time someone did, US Customs had two immigration officers processing about one thousand people (I do not exaggerate) and it took me two hours to get through!

Did you read *Bonfire – the Making Of?*† It's at once amusing and appalling, the ultimate in Hollywood indulgence stories – art mirroring life, I guess. At the heart of the trouble was that there was *no producer.* De Palma did exactly what he felt like doing at any given moment, and the studio was too chicken (and ignorant) to do anything about it.

We went to see *Money and Friends* the new David Williamson play on Friday. It's great – fast, funny and nice performances from, among others, your favourite tragedienne, Robyn Nevin. There is a long article in the Saturday *Australian* about David's paranoia about critics. It publishes a letter he unwisely sent to five theatre critics just before the play opened, and has a long and equally unwise interview with him. It seems he longs to be taken seriously. I always thought he was. I'll bring it with me. Is there anything else you want? Vegemite, Saturday's *Herald*?

Peter Yeldham just called. Apparently those boys have got Oppy well and truly convinced. Peter has had his agent ring Ken and Clayton a couple of times and got nowhere. At this stage I think

---

* Bruce had been asked to direct a film version of the stage musical.

† True title is *The Devil's Candy: The Anatomy of a Hollywood Fiasco* on the filming of Tom Wolfe's bestseller *The Bonfire of the Vanities.*

enquiry only inflates their sense of self-importance. I *do* think they are in trouble with the project because there has been nothing about their proposed documentary on the 50th anniversary of the Tour de France – due to happen last November. If they'd been there, there would have been plenty of publicity. It seems we will have to continue to wait and see.

FAX FROM Bruce to Sue, 15 January 1992

Brian Moore is going to be less than thrilled to hear that his Australian trip is off! Someone told him it was definite and he's been packing his Y-fronts ever since.

I just saw Aden and August Schellenberg for lunch. They are fine and are crashing around here looking for agents. I suggested a couple of people at ICM.

I guess you have a copy of the fax from Tristram at Majestic. No matter what he says no-one seems to know about the film as yet. Chris Kenny [producer, *Les Misérables*] hadn't heard of it opening nor had William Boyd.

FAX FROM Bruce to Sue, 15 January 1992

I spoke to Michelle Abbrecht (very dishy) at Goldwyn and she assures me (not surprisingly) that they are sending out all kinds of stuff for the Awards. It seems that videocassettes of the entire film are *not* going out, and then only to selected groups including directors. She says others can see it in the theatres. This is true, of course, but equally true of all the odd films I'm receiving every day on cassette, most of which have far less chance than *Black Robe* of nominations. *Time* magazine placed it fifth on the Ten Best list.

I can easily meet you any day except Wednesday, when we're showing the first cut of the film to Richard Zanuck.

I haven't read the *Bonfire* book but I hear it's good. Isn't that the book

I gave you? I thought if I read it first you'd be able to tell the pages had been turned.

I thought Williamson's play was good too. I read it when I was out in Sydney. I bet Robyn Nevin didn't underplay.

Poor old Oppy. I'd have thought years in politics would help him spot stuff like this. The big question that remains and that haunts me is *What on earth are they doing? Is there any point to all their meetings, travels, promises and publicity?* I think I've now got past the stage of disappointment that such a potentially wonderful film has not been made and just want to know what they were/are up to. I love working out people's motivations, but those two have me 100% baffled.

FAX FROM Sue to Bruce, 17 January 1992

Tracey is on the case re Brian. The pathetic picture of him folding his Y-fronts into his suitcase moved us all.

Yes, the *Bonfire* book was the one you gave me. By the way, Anne Whitehead got the money for the third draft of the Paraguay script. She might be getting me some notes before I leave, to read on the chairlift. On Monday I am going to see something called *Henry: Portrait of a Serial Killer* at the Censorship Review Board. It has been refused registration… oh, yuk.

FAX FROM Sue to Bruce, 14 February 1992

I have here for you a Hoyts Gold Pass – sent by Hugh. I have one also. I have coveted having one for years. I will hold yours here. If you hear that there have been sightings of Bruce Beresford around George Street, it will be Tom getting into Hoyts for free.

I have an LA acquaintance who phoned me the other day about a movie she intends to make in Queensland. She knows Max Youngstein [film producer] who told her he adored *Black Robe*, thought it was a great movie and that Goldwyns had really screwed up the release.

It was snowing as I left Aspen – very hard to leave.

FAX FROM Sue to Bruce, 21 February 1992

Dear Bruce and Virginia

We had the Sydney preview last night. It went off very well. There was absolute silence through the credits (interminable as they are) and then a burst of spontaneous applause. [Producer] Michael Thornhill (who was not invited) said, 'Good to see a well-made film for a change.' Jack Thompson thought it was wonderful and kept coming up to me grinning like a loon. I think the violence got to a lot of people, who were rather overwhelmed by it.

Lothaire and his mother arrived yesterday morning, sans half their luggage, after a marathon trip from Montreal via Chicago, where they were rerouted to San Francisco, then another change in Honolulu. Last night Lothaire took a bow before the screening then went home to bed.

I think I told you the poster is up on bus stops all over town.

Tom and I went to the launch of Roger Milliss' new book the other night – an epic retelling of a massacre of Aborigines in the 1830s called *Waterloo Creek*. Whether you want one or not, a copy is coming your way, a gift from me. I always think one should do the right thing at such affairs. We sat next to Peter Yeldham during Roger's interminable speech, and Peter said that all has gone completely silent on the Ken and Clayton front.

FAX FROM Bruce to Sue, 24 February 1992

I'm glad they are showing the uncut print of *Black Robe*. I can't get over Sam Goldwyn cutting it here; it's certainly not as violent as *Dances with Kevin* [*Dances with Wolves*].

I've been post-synching *Rich in Lurv*, went to London for a weekend(!) to do Albert Finney. Briefly saw Adam, Benjamin and Cordelia. A is at Oxford and as withdrawn as ever, B is working quite happily in his usher's job, and C is in my London flat complaining about her lot in life as usual.

We had a fairly successful test screening of *Rich in Love*. I'm a bit fed up with Lili Zanuck* who wants just about anything removed from the movie of any interest: (a) the revelation the mother tried to abort the daughter (b) the affair between one of the girls and her brother-in-law and (c) the birth of the baby in a toilet. With these incidents gone I'll have an eventless movie of the week.

The *Les Misérables* people would never give me an answer on using Peter James as cameraman, so I've had to say to them that if he doesn't do it I don't do it. I haven't heard back yet. No doubt they're having earnest discussions. I feel if I don't get the cameraman I want I'll never get anything.

Saw Barry's show being taped two nights ago. As guests he had Burt Reynolds (who told quite a funny story about Greta Garbo trying to seduce him), Sean Young, Barry Manilow and Cesar Romero, who is 86 and still working. It was pretty funny and should be a big success.

I don't suppose you've heard any more about the Lyons–Sinclair fiasco? Peter Yeldham was a *total drongo* letting them have that script without a 'make by or return' clause.

---

* Lili Zanuck, wife of the producer Richard Zanuck, had her sights set on a directing career. She directed one film, *Rush*, in 1991 but has worked mainly as a producer since that date. BB

FAX FROM Sue to Bruce, 2 March 1992

The parliamentary screening of *Black Robe* went off extremely well. Margaret Pomeranz of *The Movie Show* came down and acted as MC. The new Minister for the Arts, Wendy Fatin, made a speech carefully written for her by her department. She was followed by the Canadian High Commissioner, who said encouraging things about co-productions and regurgitated most of the press kit, thus usurping most of my speech in the process. So I said a few grovelling words about how fabulous the AFC and the FFC are, introduced Lothaire and Aden, and then introduced you. Then you came on the big screen. Your remarks were pitched exactly right, and the ending was terrific. Then the movie rolled. It all worked extremely well.

There was a party afterwards in Parliament House, which was really well attended and the Minister stayed for well over an hour.

The other Leon Fink, the one who is the Big Boss of Hoyts, was there, and we ended up drinking his Moët at the Hotel Canberra after it was all over. He is a sweet and avuncular businessman who talks and thinks nothing but money.

The Jesuit screening in Melbourne was fairly informal, with a brief introduction by a handsome and vaguely sexy Jesuit, followed by me, then Lothaire who said a few words quite gracefully. In Sydney, however, Father Greg O'Kelly, who is the headmaster of Riverview, made an interminable introduction in which he warned the audience of the shocking content of the film, explained in tedious detail the historical background to the characters and the events, and told them the caption at the end and disagreed with it! He had, of course, approved the screening of the film in the first place. I didn't wait around to find out how the audience coped.

Lothaire and Madame really enjoyed themselves. Tracey took them on a boat on the harbour, and to the Gay Mardi Gras. I had them to lunch at Bondi Mansions and Lothaire grooved around the city in his few hours off. Tracey looked after them really well. So that was a success. Aden worked very hard, did *Sixty Minutes* and four pages in a new magazine called *Who Weekly* (a magazine for morons).

So. Now on to other things. I called David Butterfield this morning. He gave nothing away. He said I should call them direct and discuss it with them. I think there is no point in making the call until you are fairly sure that *Les Misérables* is a lost cause. So let me know, and I will rehearse being charming and seductive (the former, at least, will take a little time).

FAX FROM Sue to Bruce, 3 March 1992

This morning I spoke to Ron Reuben, who was the curmudgeonly investors' representative on *Fringe Dwellers.* I asked him if he'd heard of Ken and Clayton, and he said no, nor any group connected with Bruce Small, raising money in Queensland. I said they claimed to have $100m, he said 'Absolute bullshit!' He added that if there was anything going on up there he would probably know about it.

Curiouser and curiouser.

You will be excited to hear that I just had a call from Shay Martin, asking if I knew any scriptwriters for the Chow Hayes project. I pointed out that anyone competent would have to be paid; although she assured me they have $12m for the production it seems there's nothing for the script! I put her on to John McQuaid at the NSW Film and Television office. He will now hate me for life.

TEL No.   Mar.20,92 15:34 P.01

2111 N. Bronson
Los Angeles, CA 90068
Ph: (213) 856-0679
Fax (213) 466-3922

March 19th

Dear Sue,

Georges Delerue died about an hour ago. He had a stroke minutes after finishing the music recording for "Rich in Love". It looked as if he would recover, but last night he lapsed into a coma.

He was very popular here, as everywhere, & the whole town is upset.

Love,

Bruce

FAX FROM Sue to Bruce, 26 March 1992

I am still reeling from the news about Georges. I didn't quite realise when I called that it had all happened that day. I keep thinking about Colette, how nice she is and how difficult it will be for her. I could not believe my eyes when I picked up your fax – the news coming on top of Tom's mother and Rita dying within days of each other. Tom's mother died of a stroke, and Rita had a brain tumour. Ritie was in great shape until a week before, and I'm afraid we weren't ready for it. She died on Friday, the day of Tom's mother's funeral. She was at the vet's. We got there – after a church service in Sydney and trooping down to Bowral for the burial – but she had died only minutes before. As you know she was never more than two feet away from us and there is a terrible gap – it's very hard to get used to. It's no use saying she was just a dog because of course she was not. So things are pretty glum around here at the moment.

Thank you for sending me the new Goldwyn poster which is light-years ahead of their first effort and, no doubt, came too late. Interesting that they copied the Australian design, but still couldn't help themselves and overdid it.

Turtle Beach opened last Thursday. Apparently there were no preview screenings for the press. The *Herald* reviewed it this morning: 'Turning Turtle'. Lynden Barber did a real job on it. The *Sunday Telegraph*'s review is 'Turtle Beach Lays an Egg'. David Stratton gave it half a star (he seemed to have the hots for Joan Chen) and Margaret two and a half. Stratton let Stephen Wallace off the hook, saying he couldn't have been totally responsible because he wasn't around for most of post-production.

I hope in spite of everything you had a good week's skiing, and there was plenty of snow. In January we stayed at the Aspen Club Lodge, right across the street from the gondola. It was in the Lodge Restaurant (where we used to have our muesli) that Dewi Sukarno hit one of her socialite rivals in the face with a broken champagne glass on New Year's Eve, resulting in a multi-million-dollar lawsuit. Nothing so exciting happened during our stay.

One of your NZ interviews seems to carry an unwitting scoop, about your pulling out of *Les Miz.* Is it now official? If so, what does this mean so far as your geographical location is concerned? Not to mention future projects.

Richard Soames, the Film Finances big boss, is here so I have been quite busy. I'm off to New Zealand on Monday to go round the traps. I can't say my pulse is racing at the thought.

I guess your mix will be a bit emotional without Georges. I feel sure he will be around somewhere, baton in hand, when the music goes in.

FAX FROM Bruce to Sue, 2 April 1992

Sad news about Tom's mother and poor old Rita going at the same time as Georges Delerue.

Two days after he died we headed off for Aspen, which I agree is marvellous. I spent the first week in bed with ghastly flu. Benjamin had to ski alone. Trilby had lessons every day and ended up going down the black slopes.

I thought I'd told you I was out of *Les Misérables.* The crunch came when it became necessary to appoint a cameraman as he would be needed in June for location surveys. Cameron [Mackintosh] had been stalling me for two years over Peter James, endlessly suggesting alternatives – the name changing according to whoever had recently shot a hit film. Finally he said he wouldn't use Peter but wanted a cameraman who could have 'the relationship Young had with Lean, Storaro with Bertolucci'. What a load of crap! I think Young's work is old-studio style and I am tired of Storaro's endless sunset scenes. Knowing that my work with Peter, visually, is as good as I've ever achieved, I realised we couldn't possibly come up with anything that would satisfy him, so best to pull out early. I quit. In the last couple of weeks he's offered the film to John Schlesinger (who called me) and Andrei Konchalovsky.

I'm now on the point of doing a deal with Zanuck/MGM on Horton Foote's script about Bessie Smith, which I've been holding onto for over three years. It's a tricky subject (all black cast, etc.) but there is a lot of enthusiasm and the plan is to film in February. We go to Europe at the end of this month, once I have the print of *Rich in Love*, and will perhaps rent a place in the south of France where I'll work on the *Bessie* script rewrite. Horton Foote is a writer of genius but has no idea whatever of construction or how to make scenes effective without dialogue, so I have a massive editing job on my hands.

Since the news of my disassociation with *Les Miz* leaked out I must've been offered 50 scripts (very flattering) and a couple of really good ones, including a marvellous western with Harrison Ford. But I can only make one film at a time. Naturally, I'd prefer to make all my movies with you; as it's no doubt not possible, let's try and do as many as we can. *Get that bicycle number off Clayton and Ken!*

I know that *Black Robe* hasn't taken the money of *Driving Miss Daisy* but I get calls and/or letters every day from people who found it so affecting that they want me to do a film for them. I've never looked at any of my old movies, but I still think it's the best thing I've done. It's full of passion. The contributions of Lothaire and Delerue are immeasurable and will grow with the passing of time.

I'm not surprised at the reviews of *Turkey Beach*. I was asked to look at the footage at one point to see if I could help. There wasn't anything I could do as there was so little that could be added. A whole lot of critical scenes don't seem to have been written let alone filmed. I don't know what went wrong. Stephen Wallace did a great job on *Love Letters from Teralba Road* and *Stir*. Maybe his heart just wasn't in this film, or he was overwhelmed by production problems. That can happen so easily and the director can change from an artist into a traffic cop.

Barry has taped three more shows for NBC and I think he's going to be a success. He's as bright and charming and funny here as he is in Australia, and I think it's possible he's going to be just as celebrated.

FAX FROM Sue to Bruce, 14 April 1992

Peter won the ACS cinematographer of the year and the golden tripod for best feature for *Black Robe*. It's great for the film and for Peter.

We tried to arrange a meeting with Ken and Clayton. Chris rang on Friday to make an appointment for me and was told by a man who answered the phone that they were both out of the office. Later in the day the secretary phoned to say they were overseas and she did not know when they were due to return. On Monday morning when I was in Melbourne, I phoned their office and got Ken! He said they were just back from Kuala Lumpur and were pretty exhausted but they could see me that morning (it was 11 am when I called) and were going home to rest in the afternoon. I couldn't go right then because of other meetings. I asked how *A Chance for Glory* was going and he said, 'Oh, coming along, coming along.' I said I'd call next time I was down and he said very cheerfully, 'Sure, come and see us. Love to see you.'

So I will.

I have just spent a magical weekend with Evanne and her horses on the Bogong High Plains in Victoria, where she is shooting *The Silver Brumby*.* She has a baby wombat which loves to kiss you, which Trilby would adore.

FAX FROM Bruce to Sue, 15 April 1992

Have you found an adorable little pup to replace Rita?

Keep me posted on the Sinclair and Lyons drama. Talk about baffling!

---

* Evanne Chesson, leading film horsemaster and an old friend. SM

Lili Zanuck has been phoning Herbert Pinter asking to design her new film – but I know there's no finance yet.

FAX FROM Sue to Bruce, 21 April 1992

We are on the hunt for something gorgeous in the dog department, not to replace Rita because that would be impossible, but to fill the gap. We went to a cattle dog show on Sunday, where the animals were adorable and the humans quite awful. Nothing came of that. I've just advertised in *The Land*. Be prepared for lots of very cute photographs when we do find one.

I saw *Meeting Venus* yesterday which I greatly enjoyed in spite of an often jarringly clichéd script and a ferocious twitcher sitting next to me whose breathing sounded like heavy snoring.

FAX FROM Bruce to Sue, 30 April 1992
Los Angeles

I'm leaving on Saturday for Munich and the German opening of *Black Robe*. I'm getting out just in time, by the look of it; last night there were fires all over the city after the verdict on the bashing of the black guy on the freeway. Today many stores are closed and there's a lot of damage. I had to drive down to an electronics shop to get some batteries for my amazing Wizard 64KB (no, it doesn't run on beer) but couldn't get in as it was being looted by dozens of people – mixed black, Spanish and white. The whole thing has turned into a picnic with big presents for everyone. The National Guard is taking a hell of a long time to arrive.

Rich in Love is all finished. I think it's quite a good film but won't be easy to sell. No sex or violence.

John [Duigan] has had a rough time here with various projects falling apart. Goldwyn has played silly buggers with him for months. I hope he gets the Lindsay thing off the ground – with your help.*

I have to do a major revision on the *Bessie* script over the next month. But it's a great project.

I hope you've got a new wittle doggie. I love dogs and am sorry I'm not settled enough to have one.

I thought *Meeting Venus* started off promisingly, with lots of great detail around the opera company (very accurate too) but then degenerated into a soap opera story. The way the opera director was carrying on would've lost him the job in a couple of days.

FAX FROM Sue to Bruce, 1 May 1992

I saw Dick Hall the other night [Catholic intellectual, journalist and *bon vivant*]. He was telling me he was most excited to find someone else who had read the *Relations*. Seems he has several volumes. We had dinner at the Old Saigon restaurant, run by Carl Robinson, former South East Asia correspondent for *Newsweek*, and his Vietnamese wife. The dinner was arranged by Robert [Milliken] and in the group were writers Murray Sayle and Elizabeth Riddell. A very lively pair of oldies, and a pleasant change from the usual film industry crowd.

I saw *Howards End* last week. Art directed out of its mind by Luciana Arrighi, but most enjoyable, except – an alarming trend I'm noticing – about twenty minutes too long.

I'm on the trail of a new pup, which may mean an expedition to Cowra next week. Sounds promising.

I hope the opening goes well in Germany. We have had an offer of $500,000 for *BR* TV rights from Channel 7, which we will accept. Pretty good in this day and age.

---

* *Sirens* was to become an Australia / UK co-production.

FAX FROM Bruce to Sue, 15 May 1992
Braham Gardens, Kensington, London

We're settling in over here. The flat needs a lot of work and there is a lot of furniture to buy. We'll be here all June (*Bessie* work) and then will be spending a couple of weeks in July in Italy.

I was asked to write a piece on Delerue for the CD of the *Rich in Love* music. Copy enclosed. I don't know whether they're using it or not as I never had any response.

John is looking forward to working with you on his film. I've told him to expect a different kind of person to Jan Sharp.

Saw Bill Anderson yesterday. He's in London cutting Ridley Scott's *Christopher Columbus*. He has over one million feet of film and says despite that it's hard to cut it together. Ridley is really a brilliant director but is almost entirely visual. Bill says 'the actors need a lot more help'.

FAX FROM Sue to Bruce, 28 May 1992

Dear Bruce and Virginia

Attached are a few bits and pieces. I'm afraid you're going to have to accept that your place in history is going to be as Rita's director.

The good news on this front is that we have a new widdle doggie. She is a blue cattle dog, eleven weeks old, with somewhat odd markings which give her the appearance of a puzzled panda. She is, however, quite adorable and life is getting back to normal. Photos will follow.

Thanks for the reference. No doubt *my* place in history will be as 'a different kind of person to Jan Sharp'. John and I seem to be getting on fine. I hope we can pull it together, as I really like the script and I want to work with him.

I met Jake Eberts the other night. He was here to promote *City of Joy* with Patrick Swayze (who was also here but I did not meet him). I asked Hugh McGowan to arrange for me to see Jake, which he did. Jake was charming, made half an hour for me in what seemed a really tough schedule, which I appreciated. I could not interest him in John's film. Although he said he was fully committed he indicated he could always make room for a Beresford film. He's coming out here for a month at Christmas with his wife and kids. I decided not to tell him how awful the weather can be. He might be lucky.

We are having one final fling to try to get Lee Robinson the Raymond Longford Award. I'm not sure Lee will live that long, as he's pretty sick but at least we've done the right thing.

Saw *Basic Instinct* last week. Found it hollow and disappointing. I knew who done it halfway through, and the so-called scandalous sex was entirely hype (to a jaded person like myself, anyway). I think I've seen enough of Michael Douglas' one performance for a while.

from "Encore"

■ **The film industry was saddened at the recent death of one of its most popular stars Rita Milliken Jeffrey, canine daughter of Sydney producers Sue Milliken and Tom Jeffrey.**

She had worked for 14 years primarily in the production area but rising to executive status.

Offered an acting role by director Bruce Beresford, with whom she had a long relationship, she jumped at the chance and audiences fondly remember her lively truck top performance in the opening sequence of *The Fringe Dwellers*.

Show business was in Rita's blood and she was named after the voluptuous femme fatale Rita Hayworth, also a redhead. RIP.

FAX FROM Bruce to Sue, 14 June 1992
London

Lenny Hirshan is in London and mentioned the business of Hugh McGowan's acquiring the Australian rights to *Bessie*. He said he has the impression that MGM are interested and wants Hugh to contact Alan Ladd Jnr direct. Can you pass this on?

It's Trilby's birthday today and about 25 little monsters are about to descend on this partially constructed flat. I think Adam, Benjamin and Cordelia are coming too, as well as Barry Humphries and Tessa.

Next Friday I go away cycling with Adam in Brittany for six days. Hope I'm up to it.

I'm expecting William Boyd's script of *A Good Man in Africa* in a few days.

I don't suppose there are any further developments with the utterly mysterious team of Lyons–Sinclair? I find I still lie awake at night trying to work out what they were up to.

FAX FROM Sue to Bruce, 16 June 1992

I passed the information from Lenny on to Hugh, it seems MGM would talk a deal with Hugh, and if he can compete with UIP [film distributor] for the territory, they might go with him.

Lyons–Sinclair are completely, utterly silent. I was going to visit them last time I was in Melbourne, but I was feeling really crook from an encounter with a horse in which I came off second best, and it was all I could do to stagger from one essential appointment to another, then limp home.

FAX FROM Bruce to Sue, 16 June 1992

The budget of *Bessie* is around $20m and we start shooting in February.

Barry Humphries has done a short TV series for BBC and seems fine.

The Cambridge Film Festival(!) is running a BB retrospective and have *Fringe Dwellers*. They're trying to find 35mm prints of *Don's Party* and *The Getting of Wisdom*.

Cordelia is going to USC film school. I'm not saying anything to her but I think it's a mistake. C is *very* smart with excellent taste, but these are not essential requirements for a career in the film industry.

We look forward to photos of Rita II.

FAX FROM Sue to Bruce, 17 June 1992

I will keep you posted how Hugh goes with MGM.

I guess you have heard about Brett Whiteley. Found dead in a Thirroul motel room, opposite Wyewurk.* Suicide seems unlikely. According to the papers he used to go there to dry out before an exhibition. This time, perhaps his system couldn't take it.

I hope Cordelia will be happy at USC. With so much beauty and brains, there must be something she can find to challenge her. Tell her to beware the bullshit factor.

The pup is now known as the canine cannonball.

FAX FROM Sue to Bruce, cc Martin Meader and David Giles, 1 July 1992

When I was in Brisbane recently I was approached by two young Brisbane producers, David Giles and Martin Meader, about a project they hope might interest you. They played me the enclosed tape, and I was sufficiently moved by it to offer to pass it on to you. The woman's voice introducing the music is that of Vivian Bullwinkel,

* Wyewurk, the house where D. H. Lawrence wrote the novel *Kangaroo*.

the WWII nurse who was the sole survivor of a massacre by the Japanese prior to being interned in the camp where the events of the story took place. Also enclosed is some background material about the story. There is a screenplay which I have not seen.

I think the enclosed material will be enough to evoke a response as to whether you could be interested or not in the project. If you are, I will talk further with Martin and David as to how they might proceed.

FAX FROM Sue to Bruce, 1 July 1992

The rather formal letter re *A Voice Cries Out* is to show to the two boys in Queensland. They of course want to produce this film themselves, having never, so far as I am aware, produced anything. The project is, at least, interesting. Lots of good parts for women!

FAX FROM Sue to Bruce, 7 July 1992

Did you ever return from your bicycle tour? We got the postcard, thank you. It looked and sounded wonderful. I hope you are not lying in intensive care in a public ward in a large provincial hospital, trying to communicate in French...

Things are quiet here, the quietness broken only by an outbreak of public attacks on John Morris and the FFC by producers pissed off with their high-handed attitude. There have been public calls for John's resignation and not too many calls for him to stay. I'm not sure where it will end, it will depend I think on new appointments to the board, which the government seems in no hurry to make. I think they are probably sitting back and watching with interest.

The AML&F wool store, the biggest and best of the old Darling Harbour wool stores, burned down yesterday, providing an exciting lunch hour for the tourists. The fire was spectacular – all that lanolin. There is a general view that it was arson.

Tom's father died on the weekend – a month or so short of his 95th birthday and completely gaga. So everyone is relieved. Funeral tomorrow and then down to Bowral to bury him next to Tom's mother. No more for a while, I hope. There aren't any more old ones left.

FAX FROM Bruce to Sue, 9 July 1992

I'm back from the cycling tour and it was great fun. We did about eight to ten hours riding a day and I managed reasonably well, though had to walk up quite a few hills. Adam seemed to find them no trouble.

I'm waiting anxiously on Horton Foote's rewrite of *Bessie* following my notes and planning the film with Zanuck. I hope it doesn't fall through as the renovations to the flat are costing a squillion. Everything here is insanely expensive; I'd say at least three times that of the US. We need eight(!) new doors for this flat and I've just found out they're £475 *each.*

I have William Boyd's script for *A Good Man in Africa*, which I'm passionately keen to make. It's a pretty good first draft and I'm doing notes on it this week. It'd be great if you could produce. Wouldn't you like six months or so in equatorial Africa?

Yes, the old ones are gone – except John Stoddart's father, who is 93 and also gaga. He thinks it's 1923.

FAX FROM Sue to Bruce, 10 July 1992

I don't know about six months in equatorial Africa. Couldn't you get passionate about *A Good Man in Aspen*? I'm sure the script would adapt easily to the ski season.

I'm spending a few days in Melbourne the week after next, prior to a weekend at Falls Creek, and plan to creep up on Ken and Clayton.

I can just see Adam cruising easily up the steepest hills, glasses slightly awry and a smile on his face.

FAX FROM Sue to Bruce, 20 July 1992

How is Italy? Full of Italians?

Hugh McGowan sent me, in confidence, a letter he received from Clayton. Curiously, they have no address or phone number on their letterhead and it said things like 'Ken Lyons and I have been building an independent production company in Hollywood with several projects in development. In due course we hope to meet with you to open negotiations for a distribution deal for Australia and NZ.' You also should see his signature. Cecil B DeMille could be jealous.

FAX FROM Bruce to Sue, 20 July 1992
Arezzo, Italy

We're in Italy having a very relaxing holiday at Jeffrey Smart's glorious place, having spent a week in Florence. It's hot but we are doing a lot of tramping around.

A Voice Cries Out is an excellent idea and very touching; it could work despite the vast number of WWII films. However, the two guys might have a touch of the Sinclairs about them, as they seem keener on promotion than production. Why haven't they given you the script? Without a great script they have nothing. Keep me posted.

FAX FROM Sue to Bruce, 29 July 1992

I will pass on a suitably edited version of your responses to the two boys in Queensland. They are not in Ken and Clayton's league, but are naïve. I will let you know re the script, which I did attempt to extract from them, as I did not want to burden you with it if the idea did not appeal.

The skiing was great in Falls Creek with one still clear day of such dazzling perfection that it made up for the rest. Falls Creek is expansive and beautiful, with views to the Bogong High Plains, Mount Feathertop and Hotham. Modestly I am skiing rather well, and in spite of the usual Australian hazards of sheet ice, rocks and occasional grass managed to stay upright the whole weekend (apart from sleeping).

The industry has suddenly picked up and we have a lot of projects to guarantee. Also, I have been asked to chair a review of the Western Australian film industry. With the SAFC review having had such a spectacular effect, I could not resist this challenge when offered.*

FAX FROM Sue to Bruce, 7 August 1992

One of the producers of *A Voice Cries Out* called last week. The conversation did not go terribly well because for the first minute or so I did not have a clue who he was, and he said things like, 'So, have you heard from the great man?' which, you will forgive me, did not ring any bells either.

Anyway, he told me they have all the money, from South East Asian sources (sound familiar?) and they want to shoot in February. I told him you had another engagement at that time, but that we would be interested to read the script. However he seemed to lose interest when he learned that you were not hanging around just waiting for them, and off he went.

FAX FROM Bruce to Sue, 7 August 1992

It seems the guys with *A Voice Cries Out* can't be too serious. I don't believe they have the money from anywhere without a director or actors. The film would be expensive so who would be so foolish? It's

---

* The review resulted in major changes at SAFC and John Morris' resignation as CEO. SM

a repeat of Sinclair and that lady who had South-East Asian money ($12m!) for Chow Hayes.

I did tests with two potential Bessie Smiths in LA. Acting was good, but I'm worried about anyone being able to *sing* the role. It might all fall through.*

Barry's autobiography [*More Please*] is out. Seems very well written.

FAX FROM Bruce to Sue, 17 August 1992

Thanks for the birthday greetings. We keep my age quiet from now on!

I've been thinking about Sumner Locke Elliott's last novel, *Fairyland* – based on his own experiences in Sydney in the 1930s and 40s – and I am sure it would make a wonderful film. Have you read it? If not, could you grab a copy and do so? (I can't even find my paperback in the mess of this flat or I'd send it.) An option wouldn't be expensive, I don't think, and it could be a nice Australian–American project. The action shifts to America when the hero falls in love with a US serviceman. It's a delicate work, but direct and incredibly honest.

FAX FROM Sue to Bruce, 17 August 1992

The AFI have sent us your nomination certificate for *Black Robe*. Do you have a room in your house for such things? (I know you left the Canadian award in your hotel room, but these are quite nice.)

I'm off to WA tomorrow. I am chairing a committee of representatives of the WA guilds and unions who will no doubt all be pushing different barrows. It should be fun.

---

* It did, though a test sequence was shot with Queen Latifah. The studio people who viewed it commented 'That fat black girl will never go anywhere'. Less than two years later Queen Latifah was world famous. A TV film was made of *Bessie* in 2014 with Latifah in the eponymous role. Sadly, Horton Foote's script was not used. BB

I'm looking forward to Barry's autobiography. Does it cover the episode where Diane cut up all his suits?

There was something in the paper here a couple of weeks ago about your having chosen a Bessie. I suppose the recordings of Bessie Smith are not good enough to use – somehow it's never the same with another voice.

Are you interested in the Cowra Breakout? I'm being sent a script that I reluctantly said I would read and advise the writer on someone to help him with it.

PS. Just got your note about *Fairyland*. Have not read it so we are acquiring a copy.

FAX FROM Bruce to Sue, 18 August 1992

I wrote a script on the Cowra Breakout, but abandoned any idea of a film when the TV series was made.

FAX FROM Sue to Bruce, 31 August 1992

A Voice Cries Out. Herewith a letter from the two Queensland guys.* I have never been asked to sign one of these things before, and I'm not starting now. Unless you are particularly keen to read their script, I'm of a view to tell them to shove it (nicely, of course). What do you think?

A Chance for Glory. I finally ran across someone who knows all about Ken and Clayton! I was visiting the set of a movie in Melbourne for Film Finances. As I was leaving one of the actors said, 'Whatever happened about *A Chance for Glory*?' It seems he knew Clayton when he (Clayton) was an advertising producer, and talked to him

---

* The legal letter required that the signatory agree not to disclose the contents of the script to anyone and not to reproduce it. It is sometimes a requirement of Hollywood studios on major productions.

about the idea. The actor told them to get a scriptwriter and they got a list on which was Peter Yeldham's name. Subsequently when this guy tried to become involved they told him you and I were doing it. It also seems that they did trail your name around rather extensively and finally, they got mixed up with someone in Hollywood who will take it nowhere.

I saw the mini series on the Hitler diaries in which Barry plays Rupert Murdoch. Barry is just about the best thing in it, although it did have its bizarre moments. It made me want to work with Barry as a straight actor – he looks so *normal*, which is, of course, a performance in itself.

Strictly Ballroom is nauseatingly successful at the box office, taking millions. It is great fun, although by no means a great film. But I guess everyone needs a laugh right now, and it delivers. I would like to do something lovely which makes a lot of money.

FAX FROM Bruce to Sue, 31 August 1992

This flat is slowly nearing completion, though at a colossal cost. It's depressing to look in estate agents' windows and see amazing places going for at least a third less than we paid for this.

I'm working hard on the *Bessie* script. Horton Foote has been through three drafts and it's getting pretty good now. We still don't have all the finance in place, though.

We're going to Venice this Friday for two days, as I've been roped into a film directors' conference. The agenda was faxed to me and is impossibly pretentious. It seems to be both a swipe at American studio movies and a gripe along the 'why don't they make 'em like they used to?' lines.

I think those Queensland guys can shove it up their jumper. I've had scripts sent to me from Robert Redford, Spielberg, Harrison Ford, etc., and never been asked to sign any stupid forms. Meader and Giles seem to be under the impression we're a couple of used-car salesmen. Seeing as they want to be so formal, tell 'em I'll sign the form if they supply a full financial breakdown of their company structure with a list of investors (with addresses), plus a detailed budget of the film. I would also like the validity of their finances attested to by a bank manager. This is only fair. Why should you or I sign legal agreements that are totally one-sided? We know nothing about these people. They could be living in a fantasy world and just wasting our time.

The Lyons–Sinclair stuff gets more and more mysterious. Why would they get tied up with some guy in LA when we were already in a position to set up the film? I think I told you that Guy East of Majestic loved the script when they took it to him, but was puzzled when they said they didn't want any finance. They didn't appear to want anything! They never mentioned my interest to him. Anyway, keep on the trail.

I'm sure *Fairyland* could make a wonderful film. I don't think the storyline is much of a problem until the unsatisfactory ending. The childhood stuff is reminiscent of his other works and I'd drop that. I spoke to his agent in New York, who I've met socially as she also represents Alfred Uhry, and have arranged to see her around 8 October. It might be worth my taking out an option.

FAX FROM Sue to Bruce, 1 September 1992

The flat sounds amazing. Don't be too depressed about the resale value. Good times will come again, hopefully before you're too old to enjoy them.

I guess the trick with *Fairyland* is how you approach it, and where the emphasis is placed. I don't think anyone has done the 1930s and 1940s in Sydney, that rather innocently parochial, sun-drenched society. The New York section is good also. The end of the novel is certainly very theatrical, but a more believable alternative should be possible. Would you do the adaptation yourself? Or could we interest David Williamson? Presumably, being dead, Sumner Locke Elliott would not be too fussed about necessary changes to suit a screenplay. If an option is obtainable and you want to do it, let's do it together. My caution about how it's treated is to some extent related to the prospect of financing. But I'm happy to give it a fly.

FAX FROM Bruce to Sue, 9 September 1992

Will you somehow pass on the enclosed letter to Phillip Adams regarding the videos of the movies I did with him?

It'll be great to have the SAFC ones (let me know, of course, if they charge), but will you check with them that *Money Movers* is the uncut version? They did a peculiar version for Malaysian distribution in which the ending was changed and the action modified. Amazingly, this was shown on London TV and is the one supplied to video stores in Britain.

The *Black Robe* box notes are the usual kind of trash. I still love the catchphrase on the Australian poster: 'A journey to Paradise'.

FAX FROM Bruce to Phillip Adams, 6 September 1992

Dear Phillip

I've been trying lately to find copies of all my films on video, mainly because, as the years go by, the kids ask to see them, and I find I only have a few of the American ones. Do you know if it's possible to get videos anywhere of *Don's Party* and *The Getting of Wisdom*? Would you have any idea where the video masters are now?

I hope you're well. I know you're prospering. I was back in Sydney for a few months editing *Black Robe* and often heard you on the radio. I made some attempts to contact you but your whereabouts were a closely guarded secret.

Virginia and I are fine. Our daughter, Trilby, is now six. Adam is in his final year at Oxford and Cordelia is doing a postgraduate course at UCLA. Benjamin has had an ushering job for three years at a London cinema and seems quite happy.

I've just read Barry's autobiography, in which we both rate some brief mentions. It finishes in 1973, so there'll be another volume. It's well and surprisingly soberly written, often quite funny and revealing.

I'm trying to set up a film on the life of Bessie Smith, begin filming in February. I'll be in Australia over Christmas and would like to see you. Let me know how to contact you.

Regards,

Bruce

FAX FROM Sue to Bruce, 11 September 1992

I have on-faxed your letter to Phillip Adams.

I saw Ken and Clayton's actor friend in Melbourne yesterday. He has been talking to them. He says they told him that we had asked for fees of $2m for you and $1m for me. (It was in fact $1.75m for you and $350,000 for me.) They have more or less realised that the guy they are dealing with in Hollywood, Gordon Weaver, is unlikely to do them any good, but they think they have a hot property and they don't know what to do. Clayton is afraid of losing it – Clayton wrote the original treatment which went to Peter Yeldham. They reckon they've got a $5m investor (come down a bit, hasn't it?). My friend thinks that Ken's family has money which has floated them this far. *That* figures, I must say.

I said there was no intention on our part to cut them out – that they could have an executive producer credit, and that points would be divided in reasonable proportions to all parties. We will see what happens next. I think it's best to leave it to pop and bubble away and see what happens.

FAX FROM Bruce to Martin Meader and David Giles, cc Sue Milliken, 11 September 1992

Dear Giles and Martin

Thanks for sending me your script of *A Voice Cries Out*. I know that you won't mind that I've had it duplicated and arranged for its sale around London at the tube stations.

I think it's capably written and bears the marks of detailed research, which is always an advantage. As an overall comment, however, I think it would benefit from rather fuller characterisation of the leading people. As it is now, I feel we learn irritatingly little about them, in addition to which more detail will make the conflicts in the camp more telling.

I don't think the flashbacks at the beginning add anything to the script. I doubt if you need them.

There's no doubt that it's an inspiring, if costly, project and I'd certainly like to talk it over with you when you come to London. I gather from previous correspondence that you've already raised the money for the film, so, provided your budget is realistic the most difficult task is already over. You should have no trouble attracting a first-rate cast.

Regards,

Bruce Beresford

FAX FROM Bruce to Sue, 12 September 1992

That information on Ken and Clayton makes sense in a mad sort of way. Our fees weren't high considering the budget and in any case they never objected.

I'm due back in the US on 10 October for *Rich in Love* at the Chicago festival. Then I'll be staying to begin pre-production on *Bessie*.

FAX FROM Sue to Bruce, 14 September 1992

How did Meader and Giles get a script to you so quickly?

I am mailing you today a long article in Saturday's *Australian* by Phillip Adams about his association with Barry Humphries apropos Barry's biography.

John Duigan called on Friday with the good news about *Sirens*. So we have a bit of work to do now, to see if we can get it together.

FAX FROM Bruce to Sue, 14 September 1992

Meader and Giles' script just turned up unexpectedly. I'll keep them at arm's length – the script needs a *lot* more work than they obviously believe.

Phillip Adams is one of the world's least unassuming people. As a producer he was remarkably casual – on *Barry McKenzie* he spent four days in London – just went back to Australia before we started shooting.

FAX FROM Sue to Bruce, 17 September 1992

I just had a call from Ben Gannon [producer] to say that Helen Boyd (remember…) has offered to option *The End of the Line* (now titled *The Light of Day*, which I think is better) to him. Ben told her he would only consider it if he had a straight option under the same terms as any other writer, was able to get rewrites done elsewhere, and she had no involvement in the production. She agreed. He asked if I would be interested in producing it with him, and whether you would still be interested in it. Helen Boyd sent the script to Majestic who liked it. Ben checked with them and heard yesterday that, with an approved director and cast, they would be in it. So the question is, are you still interested? If so, I'll get the latest script to you. And you could, under these new circumstances, rewrite it to your heart's content. Ironical, isn't it?

Isn't MGM paying for *Bessie*? It should be easy, with Zanuck, you and a great project.

FAX FROM Bruce to Sue, 17 September 1992

I don't know about *The End of the Line*. It's certainly a great story, but I'd need a lot of convincing that Helen was no longer involved. In any case, it looks as if I'm tied up on *Bessie* for months, though there is a chance it won't happen. If *Bessie* falls through, it might be worth my rereading *The End of the Line*.

Bessie is problematic with MGM because: (a) it's expensive, (b) has an all-black cast, (c) is a musical and they're hard to sell in non-English language territories.

I haven't heard from Phillip Adams re the videos. I received the article you sent me and might do a reply to the *Australian*. I'll have to fax it to you to fax on to them.

FAX FROM Sue to Bruce, 21 September 1992

Your letter has gone to the *Australian* this morning.

I spoke to Ben Gannon who understood your response re *The End of the Line*. I'm not sure if I really want to go back over old ground either. So let's see.

Good luck with *Bessie*. I didn't realise it would be such a hard call. I hope MGM love the script.

Phillip Adams' secretary said he would get on to the videos this week. That doesn't mean he *will*, of course.

Can you tell me who was making the doco on Lee Robinson? It seems Lee is at last to be awarded the Raymond Longford Award. This is of course Top Secret. The AFI don't appear to have any idea how to go about preparing the presentation.

THE AUSTRALIAN 23/9/92

Letters to the editor

Looking back fondly at Bazza — and Barry

PHILLIP Adams's article about Barry McKenzie was an astonishingly accurate recollection of 20-year-old events. However, it's not correct that we "finished up recruiting South Africans" in London to play Australians. In fact, we had no problem whatever in finding dozens of willing Australians in the pubs of Earls Court.

Also, I have no memory of Paul Hogan being approached by Phillip to play McKenzie's mate, Curly, or of the idea being vetoed by Barry Humphries. A few years later, in 1976, Phillip suggested to me that Hogan play Cooley in the film of Don's Party and this might be causing the confusion. (I was enthusiastic about using Hogan in Don's Party but negotiations rapidly collapsed when he asked for a fee that was more than the film's total budget.)

It is true that I wanted nothing to do with the recent re-presentation of The Adventures of Barry McKenzie but this is because of a phobia I have about nostalgic screenings of old movies. I've turned down a large number of invitations to screenings of Tender Mercies, a couple to Don's Party and even declined to go to Paris, all expenses paid, where a few of my old Australian films were being screened. I'll gladly bore anyone to death anywhere about a new film.

Finally, I'm surprised that Phillip should say of Barry Humphries "I don't like his politics", by which I can only assume he considers Barry right-wing. In 30 years of friendship with Barry I can't think of a single thing he's said or done that could justify this appellation.

For many years he expressed distaste for the one-party dictatorships in Eastern Europe (a distaste clearly shared by the inhabitants of those countries) and I was aware that this was enough to brand him as politically "right" by some members of the Australian academic world and the press, but not, I would have thought, by Phillip Adams.

BRUCE BERESFORD
London

FAX FROM Bruce to Sue, 21 September 1992

I still haven't heard anything from MGM. Maybe it's a good idea if you reread *The End of the Line* and see how you feel about it.

I can't remember the guy's name who did the Lee Robinson doco. I should, but don't. I did long interviews with Lee, though they were very heavy-going as it was almost impossible for me to feign interest in those dreary movies. Most directors, even talentless ones, learn something from film to film, so their work slowly improves; but Lee's last films never showed one ounce more technical or story skill than the first ones. I still admire him because he kept making films in Australia when no-one else was doing it.

FAX FROM Virginia to Sue, 21 September 1992

Just because you never get a fax from me, emphatically does not mean I do not pore over your despatches with rapt attention, boundless gratitude and infinite enjoyment. You are the best source of interplanetary news and gossip, not to forget the ongoing updates on business machinations, professional feuds and industry machismo – all of which I devour avidly. And all written in a racily lucid style that makes me think you'd be a ripper scriptwriter.

Great news about *Sirens*, it looks as if we will all be in Oz for Christmas, which is a huge treat.

Lots of love,
Virginia

PS. Can you read my writing? Bruce claims it's illegible, but this is of course nonsense.

FAX FROM Sue to Bruce and Virginia, 22 September 1992

Dear B and V

Delighted to get your note, Virginia, so thank you! I could in fact read every word except at the end of the PS: 'Can you read my writing? Bruce claims it's illegible but this is of course ....??

The *hot news* of the day is that Moya Iceton is no longer with the FFC, effective at 5.30 last night. She and a very unpopular investment executive have 'left'. There will be little mourning their departures.

Ben is sending me *The End of the Line* script. He is trying to negotiate an option with Helen Boyd. I don't think he's finding it too easy.

FAX FROM Sue to Bruce, 25 September 1992

I'm just back from Perth, have received *A Good Man in Africa* and will read it and *The End of the Line* script over the weekend.

While in Perth I bought Barry's book for Tom's birthday. Cruising through it I noticed that Barry gives Phillip A. only one scant mention in the section on Barry McKenzie.

FAX FROM Bruce to Sue, 2 October 1992

I saw the two guys from Brisbane yesterday. They're very pleasant blokes and told me they have $15.6m to do the film! But careful questioning reveals they don't actually have anything but hope. They've done things like 'talked to the Australian treasurer'(!) and 'businessmen in Singapore'. I'd like to see the project go ahead, though the script needs a lot of work.

I'm going to the US for *Rich in Love* and *Bessie* meetings. I've just done a huge rewrite on the script but don't know if it's improved.

FAX FROM Bruce to Sue, 9 October 1992

I'll be at the LA house from Monday. It looks as if *Bessie* is doomed – no-one wants to do it!

I'm just sick of *Light of Day*/*The End of the Line*. Can't face it any more.

FAX FROM Sue to Bruce, 12 October 1992

There is no escape from the faxes.

I have told Ben Gannon no on *The End of the Line*. I'm not too sorry – apart from us not working together – while it's a great story, it *is* a little bit old-fashioned, and the script still has quite a lot of problems.

Doesn't sound too promising about *Bessie*. Bad news, huh. Maybe something good will happen while you're in LA.

We are still having a bad time with *Sirens*. Majestic won't agree to what the FFC wants, and I fear the FFC will reject it. They are very stubborn, as you know, and I'm told won't budge on this particular point. In any event, if I don't get it through at the next meeting we can't start at the end of February, and then we'll lose Sam Neill and the weather. Why is it always so difficult?

I'm enclosing a quite interesting piece by David Stratton from this weekend's *Australian*.

Extract from the *Australian*, by David Stratton 'On-screen sparkle dulled by dim-witted judging', October 1992

Sometimes there are obviously deserving pictures, actors or directors.

But often even film critics, whose job it is to guide the general public in the direction of the cinema's best productions, can't agree on the merits or otherwise of a film.

In the era of co-productions, the situation becomes even murkier. In terms of cinema excellence, who could bypass Bruce Beresford's magnificent *Black Robe* for the big prizes this year?

The Canadians could not, and the film already has scooped the Canadian Film Awards.

And there's the rub: fine as it is, most people would consider the film to *be* Canadian, which it is in terms of content and therefore not in serious contention for Australian awards. Though it is inconceivable that Peter James won't be awarded a prize for his exceptionally fine cinematography.

FAX FROM Sue to Bruce, 19 October 1992

It won't surprise you to learn that we did not win any of the big ones at the AFI Awards on Friday. In fact the only one we did win was cinematography. I thought we should have won sound and music – Georges' score was light-years ahead of all the other nominations – but everyone knew that. All the critics said that *Black Robe* was the best film. So everyone knew *that* as well. The real truth about the AFI awards is that they always go to the small alternative film, and never to anything mainstream.

Having said that, it was a good night. The show itself was well produced and Ernie Dingo was one of the presenters. Jill Robb and I presented the Raymond Longford Award to Lee Robinson – who could not come because, in his words, his doctor had grounded him. He has emphysema and other complicated chest problems, and could not fly. I wrote our introduction which everyone thought was pretty good. The AFI found a clip from *Walk into Paradise* which was astonishing in its crisp, bright colour. Penn [Lee's son] collected the award on Lee's behalf.

Ernie told me that *Fringe Dwellers* is the most watched videotape in all the Aboriginal communities in the Northern Territory, Queensland, etc. He said they all love it. So even if it's not making us rich, it's nice to know that. I got a tape dubbed off for him when we were doing yours.

Apart from that I'm still flat chat – busier than a bricklayer in Baghdad or George Bush's campaign manager. I'm off to Coober Pedy tomorrow to visit the mini series *Stark* which is being directed by Nadia Tass, and which has just parted company with its art director. Then on to Perth to deliver my draft report for the WA Film Enquiry.

We are still trying to get some sense out of Guy East on *Sirens*. It ain't easy. Sarah Radclyffe is on board now as the English co-producer so it will be good to see if she can eyeball Guy and get the concessions we need to get the deal through the FFC.

FAX FROM Bruce to Sue, 20 October 1992

Thanks for the fax re the awards. At least Peter won. I saw *Strictly Ballroom* in Denver and liked it a lot. It's an old story, but the setting is novel. The direction is *wonderful*. They deserve all the success they get.

No luck on *Bessie*. No-one is interested. I'm now trying to get up *A Good Man in Africa* as an alternative and am so far getting rejections even with the proposed cast of Kenneth Branagh, Sean Connery, Michael Caine and Danny Glover! Times are tough and *A Good Man in Africa* is perceived here as a 'foreign' movie.

I've had meetings re *Indian Summer* and will probably do that next fall.*

What about this fax [enclosed] from Meader and Giles! I've heard no more yet.

I'm going to New York to see about *Fairyland*.

---

* The title *Indian Summer* wasn't used as there had been so many films called that. The script – his first – was by Akiva Goldsman, who went on to become a highly successful scriptwriter and director. The film was retitled *Silent Fall* and made with Liv Tyler (her first film, she was only fifteen) and Richard Dreyfuss. It was a major flop. BB

FAX FROM Martin Meader and David Giles, Planet Pictures, to Bruce, 15 October 1992

Dear Bruce

Everything is now in place financially. We wish to negotiate on a fee and sign a contract. Everything is on schedule for commencement of principal photography on 19 April 1993.

We are now in transit to Singapore.

Best regards,
Martin Meader and David Giles,
Producers

FAX FROM Bruce to Sue, 25 October 1992
Los Angeles

We are all going to Mexico tomorrow for a holiday. Virginia and Trilby will then go back to London, I'll be staying longer in LA.

Bessie is quite hopeless, but we've really only just started showing *A Good Man in Africa* around. Dodi Fayed (his dad owns Harrods) wants to do it, and Michael Fitzgerald claims to have already raised $15m! William Morris is checking all this out on Monday and Tuesday.

Things are noticeably tough here now, with everyone being very cautious about their investments. They'll happily plonk down $45m for Jean-Claude Van Damme and will also finance $3–4m films, but in between it's very difficult. For *A Good Man* I'll have to pin down a truly fabulous cast to get it off the ground.

Absolutely nothing more from Meader and Giles.

FAX FROM Sue to Bruce, 26 October 1992

I'm impressed by Meader and Giles – they can obviously sling millions together where no-one else can!

It's looking as though I'm coming to England next week. We don't seem to be getting anywhere with Majestic on *Sirens*, and as Guy East will be back in town then, I think the only thing to do is to go over and try to eyeball him. As well it would be good to sit down and talk to John, instead of those dreary night-time telephone calls.

I was in Coober Pedy last week for a couple of days. They had had four inches of rain and the desert looked like Windsor Great Park. Beautiful, but the film people were tearing their hair out.

FAX FROM Bruce to Sue, 18 November 1992

Sorry about the silence. I'm back from LA but am still busier than Madonna's investment adviser. I have an option (free) on *Fairyland* and intend to write the script myself.*

Thanks for the info on the tapes. By the way, I finally had a long correspondence with Phillip Adams, prompted by his anger over my letter to the *Australian* and various issues in Peter Coleman's book. I'll fax some of it to you.

LETTER FROM Bruce to Phillip Adams, 4 November 1992

Dear Phillip

It's wonderful. After not hearing from you for years I get two letters in one day.

Thanks for the information on the films. I'm glad to hear about *The Getting of Wisdom* negative going to the National Library, but what about the *Don's Party* negative? Or is it already there?

---

* I never got around to the *Fairyland* script. BB

You mention organising reissues of both films, so I guess you have master tapes of both. I certainly would love to see both films reissued as I'm very proud of them, greatly treasure the time I had making them, and would like to have them seen by a new generation.

You are quite right in discounting the validity of those who told you I said you were 'behaving corruptly in the Australian Film Commission, lining your pockets with taxpayers' funds'. I haven't been in Australia for years and wouldn't have the remotest idea if this procedure was even vaguely possible. I frankly do have a lot of anecdotes about you (and Barry and David Williamson and just about all the other colourful characters I've worked with), but they all relate to personal experiences. I have no speculative anecdotes about what you've been doing since I last saw you, and that's been many years.

I don't remember you proposing that Paul Hogan play 'Curly'. You may be right, but I just don't remember. I do distinctly remember, though, talking to John Cornell on the phone and him telling me that he wouldn't consider Paul doing 'Cooley' in *Don's Party* for less than $250,000. He was appalled when I told him we were paying each actor a flat $400 per week!

I might have made jokes about using South Africans in the McKenzie film, but I'm sure we didn't use any. It's always been a complaint of mine that when filming with Australians they broaden their accents, often to the point of incomprehensibility. John Clarke is not Australian, but is an antipodean. By the way, Barry's support of and friendship with John shows that he has no blanket loathing of other comics.

I think that Barry's 'detestation of left-wingers' was reserved for those of the mindless left who couldn't recognise a dictatorship when it was staring them in the face. I remember that you used to be pretty good at spotting those guys yourself. Actually, the politician I most vividly remember Barry lampooning was Malcolm Fraser, whom he couldn't stand.

You talk in your letter about the left-wing as if it's the repository of all wisdom. I always regarded myself as a democratic socialist, and came in for some nasty shocks in England. In 1968 a group of us in the ACTT tried to send a telegram of support to the Czechs at the time of the Russian invasion. The union refused as they didn't support 'counter-revolutionaries'. A couple of years ago Bernardo Bertolucci and a group of Italian left-wing mates rushed to Prague to hobnob with Havel when he became chief of state. Where were these guys all those years Havel was in gaol or under house arrest, pleading, through smuggled letters, for the support of western intellectuals?

I don't think my arguments with *Time Out* made me 'bitter about the left'. The magazine was printing a lot of rubbish about the BFI at the time and my argument was with them.* It has never occurred to me to apply my experiences to other groups. I'm not so stupid as to think the left is always wrong – or always right.

I don't have Peter Coleman's book here so can't check exactly what he has written, but I did not say to him that you sought investment from an anti-Semite. When Peter was writing the book he had already heard the story, from somewhere or other, about me having an argument in your office with some lawyer. I confirmed that it was true and told him I met this man (whose name I don't recall now) in connection with raising finance for *The Getting of Wisdom*. At one point he and I got into an argument about the Holocaust, which he told me hadn't happened and was an invention of the Jews. This made a tremendous impression on me at the time, as I'd never heard anyone say this, and, in view of all the evidence, it was like someone announcing that the pyramids were never built. I don't know what

* I worked at the British Film Institute (BFI) from 1966–71. I was in charge of the Production Board, which was set up to help filmmakers with their first films (during an era when the film union in England had a 'no recruitment' policy; this prevented aspiring directors from entering the industry). The BFI started the careers of Ridley and Tony Scott, Mike Leigh, Stephen Frears and many others. BB

your connection was with him, but I never thought you were anti-Semitic and have never made any such allegation.

I never said you 'physically beat me up' either. Again, Peter had heard from somewhere that we had a row in your office. We did, too, and I think it was over the fact that I'd argued with the lawyer, while you were keen on retaining his goodwill while we raised money for the film. I remember us pushing each other and yelling. I didn't think much of it at the time as our relationship tended to be rather volatile, and it certainly didn't affect our friendship – *but*, over the years the story of that row has got around (the staff in your office were shocked at the time, I know), and became embellished. I've heard it quoted back at me from various sources, most of whom must've heard it tenth-hand.

I'll talk to Peter Coleman about that section of the book. I don't know about other inaccuracies, but whenever I read someone's account of events in which I was involved they always recall them differently and, it seems to me, wrongly. Look how we've been arguing over the McKenzie events. Many of the things described in both Barry's and Clive James's autobiographies are not as I recall them.

I'd like to see you, if you can bear it. As I said before, I'll be in Australia at Christmas.

Regards,
Bruce

FAX FROM Sue to Bruce, 19 November 1992

Where are you? You've been very quiet. See attached re the videos.

John's picture grinds on, up one day, down the next. We lost Majestic, now waiting to hear if a German company called NEF2, found by Sarah, will replace them. If they do, it will actually work out better. But it could fall apart again tomorrow. Not exactly news to you, I guess.

I'm off to Wellington for the weekend. The very thought will probably make your pulse beat faster. Even worse, a producers' conference. Robert Lantos might be there.

FAX FROM Sue to Bruce, 23 November 1992

Thanks for the letters, which caught up with me in New Zealand. I greatly enjoyed the correspondence with Phillip Adams.

NZ was pretty unexciting. That's like saying dog bites dog. Wellington is breathtakingly beautiful, but was also grey and very cold. Helen Watts and I went over to schmooze NZ producers for Film Finances. Next weekend is the SPAA conference in Canberra. The highlight is a formal dinner in the great hall of the new parliament house. Also there is a Rembrandt to Renoir exhibition on at the National Gallery. It's from the San Francisco galleries, which sent their treasures on tour while they restore their buildings after the earthquake.

FAX FROM Bruce to Sue, 24 November 1992

I'm in endless meetings at the moment re *A Good Man in Africa*. We just put in an offer to Sean Connery.

Barry has been half-offered a US TV series and is trying to get them to confirm it. Those big networks mess around forever.

I saw Guy East today who said he was sorry about *Sirens*, but that it was reasonable his company should take their money out first. He admires John's work and really seemed to want to be involved, but is limited by the fact that John hasn't made a 'commercial' film. I went through my usual spiel about how films like *Flirting* would've been marketed if they had originated in the US.

Meader and Giles are back in Singapore and are in touch occasionally. They send long faxes saying how everyone wants to invest in *A Voice Cries Out*. I'm sure they're sincere, and are nice guys, but just can't believe they know what they're doing. I'll be astonished if it comes off.

TO: BRUCE BERESFORD

FAX NO: 27-11-883. 3160

What do you suppose they are doing with it?

AUST. FILM COMMISSION

Film Development Funding Approvals

Project name	Applicant	Category	Amount($)
DEVELOPMENT			
* *A Voice Cries Out*	Planet Pictures Australia Pty Ltd	feature	50,000 *
Backing Up	Stephen Prime	feature	6,500
Broken Hill	Roger Scholes	feature	11,350
Cross My Heart	Trout Films Pty Ltd	feature	17,500
Dreamers, The	Rogue Productions Pty Ltd	feature	13,950
Happiness Box, The	Happiness Box Productions Pty Ltd	feature	14,300
Sound Of One Hand Clapping, The	Deborah Cox	feature	14,650
Tales Of Love	Eidolon Pty Ltd	feature	12,750
All Days Are Nights	Paula Dawson	documentary	9,720
Another Way?	Trish FitzSimons	documentary	4,922
Boys And Balls	Sue Thomson	documentary	12,800
East Monsoon	Electric Pictures Pty Ltd	documentary	8,010
MARKETING			
Bigger than Texas	Market Street Films Pty Ltd	documentary	3,100
PRODUCTION			
Etcetera In Paper Jam	Much Ado Pty Ltd	animation	130,000
Motherland	Kriv Stenders	documentary	270,001
Autumn Song	John Conomos	experimental	60,000
Evidence	Kathleen O'Brien	experimental	19,160
Bumps	Victoria College of the Arts School of Film & Television	short drama	3,300
Yeah Mostafa	Clop Pty Ltd	short drama	139,200

FAX FROM Sue to Bruce, 3 December 1992

I'm still busier than the Liberals trying to sell the GST, and we still don't have a deal on *Sirens*. I think John has lost all faith in me. But we are bashing away. It's quite exhausting. And even if we get the distributor in, there will be two months of total stress while the FFC board and their lawyers torture us all to death. I don't think taking up directing is the alternative. Too many people want too many answers too much of the time. Prostitution is looking attractive but now I'm too old. It's no wonder I like to go skiing. How's *A Good Man in Africa*? Having better luck than we are, I hope.

You'll be here any minute and I'm really looking forward to seeing your cheerful face. I've now finished reading Peter Coleman's book.

CHAPTER THREE: 1993-94

He just didn't hear Sharon say 'no'

FAX FROM Sue to Virginia, 18 January 1993

John has rather monopolised the resources here at the Nerve Centre with his film. (Tell Bruce that's what happens when he goes off and makes pictures somewhere else.) Not only that, we all like working with him a lot, especially as to date he has shown no inclination to play Botticelli.*

I'll be in London Thursday and Friday, probably run off my feet with Sarah Radclyffe, tying up the UK end of *Sirens*, then off to Colorado on Saturday to have my nervous breakdown in private. But I'll be back.

FAX FROM Sue to Bruce, 8 March 1993

I had a call from Brian Rosen with news of – guess who! Ken and Clayton! So in spite of the continuing horrors of getting *Sirens* before the cameras (nothing to do with John, I hasten to add), I just had to stop and write to you.

Remember I said they were tied up with an LA guy called Gordon Weaver? They all turned up in Sydney and met Larry Adler (FAI

---

* Botticelli is a favourite word game of Bruce's when location hunting, in which a celebrity must be named though the players are given only the first letter of the surname. Bruce and Virginia, because they play it all the time, are wizards at it and always win. SM

Insurance, who financed the animation film *Fern Gully*). Larry Adler immediately passed them on to Brian, who wrangled *Fern Gully* for him. Brian rang me: 'Have you ever heard of a couple of guys called Ken Lyons and Clayton Sinclair?' I filled him in, and he went to meet the three of them at the Regent.

After Gordon Weaver told him how to sell *Fern Gully* to Japan, they moved on to *A Chance for Glory*. To Brian's surprise (but not mine), they said they did not need Rodney's money – they had $100m already. Sound familiar? Brian asked them lots of questions about the project but they were very vague. He seemed to think they said they were writing a script. I guess Clayton's doing a bit of a rewrite.

Brian looked Gordon Weaver up in the *Who's Who of American Film*. He said he does have some good credits listed. But the entry concludes with 'asked to resign from Paramount while they investigated his relationship with service companies'. It was there in black and white.

FAX FROM Bruce to Sue, 8 March 1993
Melville, South Africa

Any attempt to find some logical reason for the behaviour of Sinclair and Lyons and their decisions just founders.

Interestingly enough, I had a fax this morning from Giles and Meader saying that they'll wait for me to do *A Voice Cries Out*. They give no indication of whether or not they actually have the finance. Like *A Chance for Glory*, this is a reasonably easily financeable project and it's only the quirkiness of the producers that is preventing its realisation.

We're shooting tests here at the moment. Colin Friels (who has the lead) is the only actor to arrive so far.

Just met two English girls who were mugged and robbed after being in Johannesburg only two hours. They went to the police who commented 'you're lucky you weren't killed'.

FAX FROM Bruce to Sue, 7 April 1993

Thanks for all your help in contacting cameramen.* Unfortunately, Russell [Boyd] is busy for a week or so and Andrew [Lesnie] never answered his phone – so he's probably still in China finishing the movie he's been doing there for months.

We've shot two days with the operator – a South African who seems very good – but have a Polish American, Andrzej Bartkowiak, arriving in the morning. It's been absolute hell here since the beginning of the shoot as the DOP seemed terribly unsure of himself, was terribly slow and underexposed nearly everything. We have to reshoot quite a bit, though Connery's stuff is mostly okay, with one really dodgy scene being so over-covered by an over-anxious me that we can edit ourselves out of trouble.

Glad to hear *Sirens* is going well. Please give my love to everyone.

FAX FROM Bruce to Sue, 20 April 1993

We'll be cutting out at Twickenham, near Richmond. It's not as much fun as Soho, but I guess the editor prefers it.

We're going better now with the new cameraman, Andrzej Bartkowiak (who has done six Lumet pictures, plus *Terms of Endearment* and stacks of others). He's very fast and enthusiastic.

The political scene here is dodgy, as I'm sure you've heard, but so far hasn't brought us to a halt. V and T went back to London last night as T starts school tomorrow.

Glad to hear it's all going well, though your fax was short on the nitty gritty G O S S I P.

---

* The first cameraman on *A Good Man in Africa*, a well-credited Australian, was mysteriously unable to cope with the job and had to be replaced. BB

FAX FROM Sue to Virginia, 31 May 1993

This is to let you know that I will be in London next week.* If you are talking to John, tell him British Airways have lost part of the cutting copy (it was checked through in three bags – presumably if it had been in one they would have lost the lot). We think a container was off-loaded in Bangkok because lots of other people have lost bags also. Much screaming has taken place and perspiring poms are searching the world. We should have it back in a couple of days. And yes, it *is* insured!

FAX FROM Virginia to Sue, 31 May 1993

Champers is on the ice and red carpet being drycleaned. Bruce arrived yesterday, John today from LA. Do come and stay. BB and I are going to Prague on Thursday, returning Sunday.

I hope the cutting copy has been located.

FAX FROM Sue to Virginia, 3 June 1993

I hope this catches you before you go to Prague.

Thanks for your note and the invitation to stay. I have booked into Browns Hotel as I think it will be easier for all. Also I don't want to wear out my welcome too early in the piece, as I may wish to stay for extended periods later!

The cutting copy turned up eventually, there was a panic about water damage but that seems to have fizzled. So calm has hopefully been restored.

---

* *Sirens* was filmed in Australia in April and May with post-production in London, which required all the footage to be freighted there. SM

FAX FROM Bruce to Sue, 27 June 1993
Bramham Gardens, London

Could you send me a paperback called *Peggy Glanville-Hicks* by Wendy Beckett? It's published by Angus & Robertson.

A Good Man in Africa hasn't turned out at all well. I'm not sure why, but the story never seems to get going and the characters are not at all interesting. The only excuse I can make is that all the production problems combined so that I aimed only at getting through the film and forgot to direct it properly.

FAX FROM Sue to Bruce, 28 June 1993

The girls are getting *Peggy Glanville-Hicks* for you. I am arriving next Monday and can deliver it in person. I'm sorry to hear your thoughts on *A Good Man in Africa*. Are you sure it is not your regular post-natal depression? Maybe it is time for an Aussie movie...

FAX FROM Sue to Bruce, 1 July 1993

Shock horror – another 22 hours on Qantas but it has to be done. We are hopefully locking off the cut next week.

I just received *We Survived* from a Dutch woman called Nell van de Graaff. Will try to read it before I see you.

FAX FROM Sue to Bruce, 13 August 1993

I spoke to Clayton today. He assured me that Rodney [Adler] had faxed you yesterday. I said unlikely, as I spoke to you yesterday, and you had not received it. 'Oh,' he said, 'I'm sure he's doing it.'

He rattled on about Rodney doing this and that, and I asked if Rodney was to be the lead underwriter and to do all the work on the float. 'Well, Rodney is terribly keen, terribly keen, passionate about the script, passionate about Bruce, he will be part of it, but we are talking to brokers and so on and we will have it all worked out next week. We need to find out what Bruce will accept as a fee, so that we can arrange a pay or play.'

So I said that if Bruce and I could see a proper financial plan it might be possible to sort out the fee situation and for Bruce to commit. 'Yes,' he said, 'I see that.' He said that this should all be together by the week after next and we will speak then.

There is just the faintest chance that he will get the underwriting together. If he would only tell us the real situation, it would move a lot quicker. We will see. *If* he's got something sensible and is willing to tell us, then we can go to the next step. I can always go to see Rodney Adler myself and explain the situation from our point of view.

Next week I'm going to be in Perisher. I badly need a break, so am really looking forward to it.

FAX FROM Bruce to Sue, 29 August 1993
Tremont Plaza Hotel, Baltimore, Maryland

Needless to say I haven't heard from Clayton again or his insurance guy. I had no call from the enthusiastic backer in Los Angeles, despite Clayton's entreaties to stay put as the call was coming 'within an hour'.

Nor have I heard any more from Greg Coote on the prison camp project. He sent me a letter from Mr Yap of Singapore, which was addressed to the three guys and spoke only in the most general terms of any investment in the film. I faxed Greg and said he must talk to Yap direct and judge for himself whether there is any possibility of investment from him or not. Meader Giles also enclosed a note pointing out that 'Mr Yap states he will put up $100,000 for development as a sign of good faith'. No amount of perusal of Yap's letter revealed any such statement. I've asked if there is some other letter in which this money is mentioned but haven't heard anything.

I'm working very hard in pre-production on *Silent Fall*. There is an absurd rush (in the wrong location) to get everything read to start filming on 20 September.

FAX FROM Sue to Bruce, 30 August 1993

Sorry I haven't been in touch before but following my skiing I had a week from hell with board meetings, the court case for my speeding offences and a visit from the Taxation Department. The latter has decided to pick on the film industry this year and we must have been their first visit, because they knew nothing. We bored ourselves to death being nice to them. No-one could be squeakier clean than Samson but it's like talking to a policeman – you feel guilty at the same time as wanting to slip hemlock into their Nescafé.

I had a long chat to Hugh McGowan yesterday about Ken and Clayton. He was totally bemused. He said they went all over the story again (which he didn't need at all), told him how they had been to Paris and here there and everywhere with Oppy. They dropped your name *endlessly*, and said that Graham Burke [CEO, Village Roadshow] was interested in the project! Hugh said, 'Well you should go and talk to Graham then.' They did say that Larry Adler was interested in putting in some of the money (not all – refreshingly frank of them). They told him they have spent $1m on the project to date. (One should hope this is a lie, as a million dollars of unjustifiable development costs would probably sink the financing.) Hugh said it appeared they are looking for money. This at least has the ring of reality about it.

He asked me what he should do, and I suggested that he write to them saying he was very interested in acquiring the project, and that as soon as they had a producer and director *contracted*, they should contact him again.

In regard to Meader Giles, the same applies. Why would they need another $100,000 of development when they have already had $50,000 from the AFC and God knows how much from Queensland?

Maybe in both cases they actually don't want to make the film – because then they would have nothing to do. While they can drift about in this endless development phase and drop your name to open doors, they have a purpose. There's probably a clinical name for the condition – *productus interruptus*? Anyway we'll keep on trying but it will be interesting to see who can outwait whom.

I lost my appeal on my licence so I am now known as the Bea Miles of Bondi, in and out of taxis like a flying ferret. I could have had a provisional licence for a year, but with that it's one tiny misdemeanour and you're in more trouble than Paul Keating. So I decided to take the three-month option and get it over with.

I'll be back in London in a couple of weeks for the final mix. I'm going to wait for the answer print, to see if Rank can cut the mustard like Arthur Cambridge [Australia's brilliant colour grader].

FAX FROM Sue to Bruce, 9 September 1993

I just spoke to Clayton. The gist of it seems to be that your agent said that you would not put your name to a prospectus without a proper contract, pay or play, etc., in place. Rodney Adler might have given them the flick, as Clayton said Rodney runs an insurance company and did not want to be seen fronting a film – 'it's very sensitive' – hence no letter to you. So Ken and Clayton have had a 'shift in their thinking' and decided to 'shift the budget way down'. They are now thinking 'under $10m, more like *Strictly Ballroom*'. They don't think you will be interested at that level and so they have been speaking to other directors, and have interest of course.

I said, 'Well, Bruce and I could finance the film ourselves if you would let us and there would be no need to go to the trouble of a prospectus so why don't you think about that? You could be executive producers, and be involved, get a fee and get your movie made.' He said they would think about it, but I don't think they will – they will continue to fiddle around – *productus interruptus.*

FAX FROM Sue to Bruce, 14 September 1993

Hugh McGowan called my office today to say Ken and Clayton had been back to see him and told him they plan to use David Parker and Nadia Tass and to make the film for $8m! Hugh said he would not distribute the picture and they were insane not to go with us.

FAX FROM Sue to Bruce, 16 September 1993

I suggest I write to Ken and Clayton as attached. Nothing to lose.

FAX FROM Sue to Ken Lyons and Clayton Sinclair, 16 September 1993

Dear Ken and Clayton

I am presently in London for the sound mix of *Sirens* (which I am producing with John Duigan directing). On thinking about my last conversation with Clayton, I want to reiterate that there is no need for you to use a less good director for the film, and to propose a way in which Bruce Beresford could be engaged.

As you know, Bruce loves the project and seriously wants to do it. The only impediment is a clear production plan, which is really a simple matter to arrange. The benefits to yourselves of using an Academy Award–winning director include:

1. The ability to earn bigger fees from the film.
2. A greatly enhanced profit potential.
3. Attaching 'A' class star casting to the film. Actors such as Robert Redford and Dustin Hoffman actually call Bruce to work with him.
4. Establishment of yourselves as Executive Producers respected in the international arena.
5. The best worldwide distribution for the film. As I mentioned

> to Clayton, I have just sold *Sirens* to Miramax and Harvey Weinstein has asked me to work with them again. Jake Eberts and Guy East of Majestic will always take a Beresford film. So we could put together a fabulous distribution package of Miramax for the US, Majestic for foreign and Walsh and McGowan for Australia, while still retaining creative control of the film. *No other producer/director team in Australia can deliver you the unsurpassed potential of this deal.*

In regards to locking Bruce into the picture, I propose as follows:

You enter into an agreement for Bruce to direct, myself to produce and yourselves to executive produce. We would mutually agree to settle on a budget figure acceptable to all parties after proper research and discussion with international distributors. I would guess that this figure would be approximately $10m. I have no doubt a budget of this size can be raised with Bruce, myself, the right casting and the distribution outlined in point 5 above. Bruce would agree to work with Peter Yeldham on rewriting the script and you would have consultation rights on all relevant aspects of the film. Appropriate fees for yourselves, Bruce and I would be mutually agreed between us.

I would take care of Bruce's agent and work closely with you on the financing of the film.

I do urge you to consider this proposal as it represents an unrepeatable opportunity to be associated with a major international success with the critical acclaim of *The Piano* and the financial reward of *Driving Miss Daisy.*

You should also bear in mind that the script at present is not ready to go into production. In the wrong hands, it could end up just another Australian period picture which no-one wants to see. After all the time you have spent on it, I think you deserve better than that.

FAX FROM Sue to Bruce, 20 September 1993

My letter elicited contact with Ken and Clayton. The response was a phone call from their accountant, David Butterfield. He had a copy of my letter and asked me what my proposal was. I said, 'It is in the letter.' 'No, but what do you propose?' he said. I was at a loss to know how to reply. Butterfield told me they have talked to Nadia Tass, and that they have someone willing to fund the cost of putting out a prospectus. I really think, after Friday's call, that it is completely hopeless.

FAX FROM Bruce to Sue, 26 September 1993

I'm working very hard on this untitled child molesting autistic comedy [*Silent Fall*] and am currently testing my new fax modem, so expect lots of peculiar messages from me, re-punctuated by ASCII. I've just spoken to Greg Coote and it seems that he now has acquired *A Voice Cries Out*. I've suggested making it late next year or early 1995, with you producing, of course.

FAX FROM Sue to Bruce, 27 September 1993

Good news about *A Voice Cries Out*.

I am still in London – leaving today for LA then home. I will send you all the news when I return but you will be interested to know that we are unhappy with our music and extraordinarily unhappy about the orange and brown answer print produced by Rank.

FAX FROM Sue to Bruce, 30 September 1993

I arrived back in Sydney this morning, and it's all been happening.

I stopped over in LA yesterday, and because of your fax I phoned Greg Coote, who actually took my call! We had a long chat about *A Voice Cries Out*, and he was very open with me. He immediately sent me round a copy of the script and Greg Ricketson's budget summary.

He said he was pleased I was involved, and I said we should talk about how we might work together, which we agreed we would do in a couple of weeks when he's in Australia.

On that latter point, I hope he will accept that I will be the producer. I don't line produce, and while I would work nicely with him and the Roadshow crowd, I would need to be able to run the show my way. So if we proceed, I'll need your support in sorting out my working relationship with Greg and Roadshow.*

Then this morning I had a call from Ken Lyons! He was chatty as anything, and said he knew my letter off by heart (the one putting a proposal to them). He more or less said that they would do a deal with me to produce *A Chance for Glory* but how did I think it would work, and I said they should option the project to me, and keep approval over the director so they could be sure it would be someone okay. He seemed nervous about going back to you before it was sorted out, because of all the faffing around, but he obviously wants you to direct. I told him it was a pity that they hadn't done something sooner, because something else had come up in the last week, however nothing was settled yet. He said they would come to Sydney next week and sit down and work out a deal with me.

Then Hugh McGowan called me to say Ken had been on the phone to him, and had read him my letter! Hugh said he's told them till he's turning blue how fabulous you and I are, and that he would be involved if we were.

This is the first time Ken has ever called – it's always been Clayton in the past, or David Butterfield. Also Ken said that Oppy is now saying 'How long do I have to live to see this movie?' He did say they have talked to other people, and that he would have to clear that up before doing a deal with me, which he would sort out before next week.

---

* Greg and I agreed to produce the film together. He did the money and I did the making. The production company was Village Roadshow Pictures. SM

The other news is that we had all kinds of problems with *Sirens* – the first answer print was orange, and the second mostly out of focus. The titles people can't seem to get the opticals right, and Geoffrey Burgon's music was nice, but wrong for the movie! So we have to do something about the score. Harvey now wants to test the film next Thursday in New York, so I am going over. As are John and Sarah.

FAX FROM Bruce to Sue, 30 September 1993

It's 10.30 pm and I've been up since six this morning. This film is terribly difficult to shoot, mainly because of the two kids in the leads – both in ridiculously demanding roles.

I'm sure you'll be able to get the whip hand on the producing of *A Voice Cries Out*. Greg assures me the Singapore investor is on the level.

Amazing about the call from Ken Lyons. I hadn't considered *A Chance for Glory* to be an option any more as Ken and Clayton seemed to have an agenda of their own that defied rational explanation. Of course, it's still difficult to tell if a deal could be worked out. If it could maybe they could be done one after the other. Let me know how your meeting goes.

Sorry about the music problem on *Sirens*. I guess you've heard we had to have the music totally redone for *A Good Man*. The Mexican composer wrote a good score for a different movie.

FAX FROM Sue to Bruce, 1 October 1993

I just had another long call from Ken Lyons, in which he said that when we meet on Monday week, after my return from New York, I should put to them the legal position I want. So he seems to mean it. He mentioned Oppy again, and I think the pressure might be coming from the old bloke. I'll be getting my lawyer on to it in the meantime. Why did they wait until we have written them off completely?

FAX FROM Sue to Bruce, 5 October 1993

Greg Coote called me this morning, haemorrhaging over Lenny's fax. Seems it was a lot more than he and you had discussed. The biggest problem, apparently, is the script/research cost. Mr Yap has agreed to put up $100,000 and Greg says that it would be impossible to go back to him and quadruple it.

FAX FROM Sue to Bruce, 15 October 1993

I'm back in Sydney and trying to catch up with life, which has become quite chaotic with all the travelling.

I talked to Greg Coote and explained that there was a lot of work to do on the script of *A Voice Cries Out*. He asked me if I thought you really wanted to do the film. I said I thought so – even though Lenny is not keen – that basically, you make up your own mind.

Then he raised *A Chance for Glory*. Ken and Clayton have shopped the thing around again! So now I am in the middle of Hugh McGowan, who has been really good about telling me what's going on, and who badly wants the film if you do it – and Greg, who would acquire the rights if he thought you would do it.

Following my conversation with Greg, Ken Lyons called me and offered me an option on the project! I am to fax him with a proposal. If I can get the option, I'd be in a better position to sort out how best to move forward with it. I don't think for a second that the negotiation will be simple but I'll give it a fly. If you want to be a partner in the project, let me know. It would be interesting to know, if you had a choice, which one you would prefer to go with first.

We had an interesting time with Miramax in New York. Harvey wants John to take about five minutes out of the film, which at 104 minutes it can stand. Also I think they are going to pay for a new music score, but as you know, these things are never simple.

FAX FROM Bruce to Sue, 18 October 1993

Of course, I'm terribly interested in doing *A Voice Cries Out*. I think it's a marvellous story, though I'm a little worried that World War II stories might be a tough sell. The research list doesn't appear to be terribly comprehensive, which means I could have quite a lot of research to do before rewriting the script. This sort of stuff just can't be made up. They've mentioned the book *White Coolies* a couple of times. I read this years ago and am sure it's good source material, but won't it be necessary to actually buy the rights to the book?

A Chance for Glory is also a great project… naturally I'd ruled this one out some time ago for reasons you know all too well. It too, needs quite a bit of research and rewriting, so maybe a deciding factor should be which one is it actually possible to get going. Did Ken and Clayton reply to your offer?

I hear the film [*Sirens*] went well in New York. I'd be wary of cutting – the studios always insist on this and almost invariably want the ending changed too.

FAX FROM Sue to Bruce, 19 October 1993

On the one hand the whole situation is quite tricky, and it really is not much complicated by your absence. I am being as careful as I can in trying to sort it out but I'm trying not to worry too much, as it will either work out or not, and there is only so much I can do to influence events.

The sequence to this moment on *A Chance for Glory* is that I sent the proposal to Ken and Clayton yesterday afternoon. No response yet. But this morning Clayton rang Greg Coote asking *him* to make an offer. In other words, now that they have my offer on the table, they were trying to ante up Roadshow. Greg told him he was carrying on 'like a two-bob hooker' and this industry being so small, Clayton need not think we all didn't talk to each other. Greg put him off till he spoke to me.

Feeling pretty terrible about the lovely Hugh McGowan, I told Greg what my offer was and, to cut a long story short, Greg is going back to Clayton to make an offer which is not quite as good as mine. If this works out, I would wind up with the option, with a gentleman's agreement to work with Greg – who says he could provide development funds.

On the matter of *A Voice Cries Out*, it's really my fault Greg hasn't been back to you/Lenny, due to the many quandaries. He is very keen to go ahead with it, and especially to land Mr Yap's investment. So I think, now that we have talked today, he will contact Lenny asap.

Nightmares with Harvey Weinstein! You were, as ever, right.

FAX FROM Sue to Bruce, 27 October 1993

This morning Ken called and it seems that *he* has finally realised that he and Clayton are parading through the town starkers. They have, said Ken, 'taken a horrible nosedive' and their creditors are pressing for payment. They are trying to find a way to get more money out of the project than I am offering. David Butterfield is still trying to put the film together with Nadia Tass.

I explained to Ken that the only chance they ever have of realising any substantial return from the project is if there is an 'A' director like yourself attached to it, so that a budget big enough to contain the numbers I offered can be raised. I also explained that any financiers would closely examine the budget and reject any unjustified development expenses.

I said that he has a window of opportunity on yourself, which almost certainly will not be there in a year's time, or even six months' time. That they should move quickly to make a decision and sell me the option. He appeared to understand all this, but still seems to be in a muddle. I think perhaps he was hoping that if he gave me the sob story I might make a better offer. But as the only thing that will get him out of the shit is $300,000 in cash paid now, it was a faint hope!

We have had a terrible time with Miramax over the extra work on *Sirens*. I think it's resolved now, but Sarah and I are exhausted. John is as happy as a kid in a kindergarten, oblivious to what we've been going through. I guess you would agree that that is what producers are for.

FAX FROM Bruce to Sue, 28 October 1993

A very interesting fax about Ken and Clayton. I'd like to have all the correspondence between us about them published.

I haven't heard anything more from Greg re *A Voice Cries Out* and still think that *A Chance for Glory* could load us up with all kinds of problems. Still, as I said before I feel almost equally keen about both of them so suppose it'll be a matter of which is really possible.

I think it would be difficult to make *Chance* for less than $25m – so can't imagine how Ken could be negotiating with Nadia Tass to do it for $8m. It's just not a subject that will lend itself to being done too much on the cheap. Not with all those cycle races and the period setting.

FAX FROM Sue to Bruce, 29 October 1993

Greg rang this morning, he reckons he's got Mr Yap's money tied up. The rest should be easy…

I'm attaching a letter to Greg for your interest, which covers the latest call from Ken. He is grasping at straws. Greg is going to get Mark Geremia [the Village Roadshow Pictures lawyer] to ring Butterfield next week. I'd love to have a tape of the phone call. I had also thought about a book – I think our correspondence probably has more potential than Oppy's story. I plan to edit it in the sun after Tom has passed on.

Under the circs, we should probably give *Voice* a fly, see if a really good script can be extracted from the material. It would be wonderful to do a really deep and perceptive film about a cast of women. And that music *is* wonderful.

FAX FROM Sue to Bruce, 26 November 1993

I'm off to London tomorrow night. I'll call Virginia but not sure if she's there or with you.

Is it true you're on to your *third* score for *A Good Man in Africa*? We are recording Rachel Portman's score for *Sirens* next week. If it's no good I'm going to kill myself. I *couldn't* go through all that again! (Studio executives screaming at you about what *they* want the score to sound like.)

FAX FROM Sue to Bruce and Virginia, 9 January 1994

Attached are some notes and thoughts about the research, for consumption also by Village Roadshow.

I'm back at work today after several days holing up in Bondi while most of Sydney – and the east coast of NSW – was in flames. We came back from the farm early, and as it turned out, wisely, because we would not have been able to get back otherwise. The main northern freeway was closed from Friday to this morning. There was ten kilometres of traffic stranded on the freeway after it was closed, and people were trapped there for up to three days. You've probably seen the fires on TV. Chris Gordon was evacuated from her house at Como twice on Saturday, it is now one of the two worst-hit suburbs. On Friday Robert drove past people in Mowbray Road, Chatswood, packing their cars for evacuation. He said they had a look of disbelief on their faces. The smoke was so thick you could hardly breathe. Tony Buckley was evacuated from Film Australia on Friday night, he said Eton Road was like a war zone, with trees exploding in fireballs all around them. The smell of smoke was right through our house on Friday night, and I had to keep cleaning blackened gum leaves out of the dog's water bowl.

Tell John the fire almost got the Norman Lindsay gallery this morning, it came right up to the garden but the firefighters stopped it.

Apart from all that, we have had a good break. The farm was beautiful for the first five days, perfect weather and we barbecued and swam in the sea. We visited Evanne one day, her farm is up on the Great Divide at Nowendoc. She has my mare and her very pretty palomino foal. It was magic being surrounded by about fifteen mares and their foals, all coming round to check us out. The heat has passed now and we are having clear and fresh summer days.

FAX FROM Sue to Bruce, 10 January 1994

Over the holidays I've been doing quite a bit of reading related to *A Voice Cries Out*. Chris turned up *White Coolies* and a book called *Captives*, which is an honours thesis by Catherine Kenny on Australian Army nurses in Japanese prison camps. There were only two of these camps, one in Japan and the one(s) in which our story is set. This discovery raises the question of what material we need the rights to in order to access specific events. Although the story is clearly in the public domain, I think that it would be proper and ethical to clarify the situation with the copyright holders of all four books:

> *In Japanese Hands*/aka *While History Passed* by Jessie Simons
> *White Coolies* by Betty Jeffrey
> *Captives* by Catherine Kenny
> *We Survived* by Nell van de Graaff

Incidentally, Nell van de Graaff was in another camp in Java, near Jakarta.

What needs to be done in England is to find out more about the two women who created the Voice choir – Margaret Dryburgh and Norah Chambers. Margaret died in April 1945, but I can find no reference to what happened to Norah Chambers apart from the fact that she was still alive when the music was rerecorded in 1983. Her husband was a government engineer in Malaya before the war. She may still be alive.

FAX FROM Sue to Bruce, 12 January 1994

Mark Geremia rang to say why don't I talk to 'the boys' [Martin and Giles]. He seems to think they have more information in their heads than they put down on paper. Norah Chambers died in 1987, apparently. He's arranging a contact for me. (Not with Norah Chambers.)

FAX FROM Bruce to Sue, 12 January 1994

Am I correct in assuming, from your letter to Mark Geremia, that Martin Meader & Co. have some more research material? I've contacted the War Museum here and have an appointment for 24 January.

I'd appreciate your sending me any stills of any kind you can find from *The Getting of Wisdom* and *Don's Party* as the video people here need them! They've been supplied with nothing!

FAX FROM Sue to Bruce, 14 January 1994

Chris has four B&W stills of *Don's Party* here to send you. What about your friend Richard Keys at the [National Film and Sound] Archive? Can't he help?

Attached is a letter from Mark Geremia's office. Boy, did those guys see Village Roadshow coming! What an *amazing* deal.

I have just spent an hour and a half with Martin Meader – the soon to be very rich Martin Meader. He was, I have to say, extremely pleasant, and promised to be very helpful.

They went to Jersey and met Sally Conway, Norah's daughter, who owns the copyright(?) in the music. Some of the original manuscripts are held at Stanford University.

The only non-civilians in the camp of our story were the Australian nurses. We chatted about lots of other incidental stuff – like there was only one person with a watch in the camp, everyone asked her the time, and she never lost her cool.

Apparently they approached Brenda Fricker about playing Margaret Dryburgh. It also sounds like Emma Thompson may have been scared off by the fact that they are so inexperienced. I might be wrong. But when we have a new script we should give it another go.

FAX FROM Bruce to Sue, 14 January 1994

Amazing about Meader and Co. I'd never have thought they were sharp businessmen considering how many times they could've gotten the film going but failed to. Suddenly they have mountains of research? Why didn't they let us/me have this before? Baffling. When Greg Coote gave me that folder he assured me they'd said that was all they had. I agree with your plans about visits to the camps and survivors, though I'm not exactly sure when the mix of the new film will be over.

I've been approached by Andrew Lloyd Webber about doing a film of *Phantom of the Opera*. It's tempting, though a hell of a big job. If it goes ahead my inclination is to begin pre-production on it this year (second half) with a designer, but shoot after *Voice Cries Out*. Anyway, it's tentative at the moment.

Despite an exhaustive correspondence with Phillip Adams I have had no luck at all in finding out where the original negatives of *Don's Party* and *The Getting of Wisdom* are being kept, if anywhere. Can you use your AFC contacts to do some sleuthing?

FAX FROM Sue to Bruce, 17 January 1994

Chris is checking with the Archive, etc., and will fax you separately about the snaps. We don't mind doing the legwork.

I've just spoken to Catherine Kenny, who wrote *Captives* (a copy is coming to you). Both she and Meader made the same point that the girls have been messed around over the years by the press, etc., and so one should approach them with care. Both she and Meader mentioned

Women Beyond the Wire by Lavinia Warner and David Sandilands, which is more about the civilians in the camp and apparently tells more about Norah Chambers. We are on the hunt for this.

My heart sank to read about *Phantom*. Just when I was allowing myself to get all fired up about *Voice*. (But at least you mentioned it!) *A Voice Cries Out* is going to be very demanding when you get down to it. You have to create the performances of a lifetime, and I don't think it's going to be one you can phone in.

FAX FROM Bruce to Sue, 18 January 1994

Don't panic about the *Phantom* situation. It's still a long way off and is by no means definite. Also, I've told Andrew Lloyd Webber that I'm doing *A Voice Cries Out* first. He won't be worried as he doesn't want to release *Phantom* until Christmas 1996.

I should've finished the mix of *Silent Fall* by the end of April and will be clear. God only knows what this one is like. At least it can't be worse than *A Good Man in Africa*.

I gather then that I do have all Martin Meader's research?! These guys are pretty confusing. Of course I agree we should use the original arrangements. If the ones on the Perth tape are accurate, they are quite wonderful.

The LA earthquake sounds frightful, though Virginia said she'd like to see the whole place slide into the sea. I don't feel angry about LA as they've always treated me very well. I was at Lloyd Webber's place when the news of the quake came through and he discussed it purely in terms of his cast album for *Sunset Boulevard* not being able to go ahead as the studio had lost power! I reached Kathy by phone last night.* They had a hell of a fright but our house is okay.

---

* Katherine Shaw, daughter of actor Robert Shaw, worked as Bruce's assistant from time to time.

FAX FROM Sue to Bruce, 20 January 1994

Thanks for the update on *Phantom*. I'm breathing a little easier.

I'm busier than a freeway engineer in LA at the moment, but will list the Meader research before I leave. The video he gave me is pretty good – it's a one-hour doco made by PBS, focussed around the American concert of the music. It tells the whole story, and a lot of the girls are there on screen – Vivian Bullwinkel, Norah Chambers, Betty Jeffrey, Wilma Oram and several Dutch women. I think this was done in 1985, so they are nearly all pretty much on the ball, apart from one old soul who is fairly out of it.

I'm glad your house is okay. Richard Soames says they are expecting locusts next.

FAX FROM Bruce to Sue, 22 January 1994

Thanks for the list of Martin Meader's material.

I've just finished remixing *A Good Man in Africa*, which is probably my worst film. Tomorrow I see the first cut of *Silent Fall*. This could be a harrowing week.

I hope the earth doesn't tremble while you're in LA, at least not because of the earthquake.

FAX FROM Bruce to Sue, 3 February 1994

I've spent part of last week and this week researching at the Imperial War Museum. They have some interesting unpublished diaries. There are *no* photos of women's camps, only a batch of the men's camps, probably all taken after the war ended.

FAX FROM Sue to Bruce, 15 February 1994

I spoke to Betty Jeffrey this morning. She sounds absolutely lovely – sharp as can be and totally together. I was hoping to see her in

Melbourne on Friday but she had something else planned and said she was quite tired – yesterday was the anniversary of the fall of Singapore and she had attended a reunion – 'When you've been kissed by 400 men it wears you out a bit.' Martin thinks she's 86.

FAX FROM Sue to Bruce, 22 February 1994

I have this little pile of stuff for you. There are some letters from the survivors, who all sound really nice. Also a piece from the *New York Times* about *Schindler's List*. It has occurred to me that we should use real names for the central characters, rather than fictionalising them. They are such authentic heroes and should be recognised as such.

Betty Jeffrey said on the phone that over the years journalists have rung them up and asked lots of questions – and then gone and printed whatever they liked. This won't surprise you, but it's easy to understand why it upsets these old girls. So they want the story told well and they are prepared to trust us, and I am very anxious to handle them with great gentleness and care.

Here's a quote from Betty (I spoke to her on 15 February): 'Vivian rang me yesterday. Usually when she calls, she says, "Is that you Bet?" Yesterday, though, when the phone rang and I answered it there was silence. Then Vivian's voice: "Are you still swimming?" It threw me for a minute. I thought, Has she gone gaga? But then I realised. So I said, "Are you still on the beach?" I don't know how we did it. It all seems impossible now. But I suppose we were young, and very fit.'

FAX FROM Bruce to Sue, 15 March 1994

I'm sorry to bugger you around still further. It's just that I've been working so hard on *Silent Fall* I haven't been thinking straight. Virginia and Trilby arrive here on 30 March for most of April, so I can't really go to Australia in that period. I haven't seen them for months and won't for some months to come, so a trip away wouldn't be tactful. I'll have to try to visit Oz in May some time.

Sirens is doing very well here and is widely admired. I was at a party last night and at least six people came up and told me they thought it was superb. Somehow they'd got the idea I'd directed it!

FAX FROM Sue to Bruce, 16 March 1994

I am in Melbourne today and I have just come from meeting Betty Jeffrey, who is really lovely. More of that anon.

Chris just read me your fax, and I am a little bit relieved because it now seems we will open *Sirens* on 28 April and I will be totally tied up for the two weeks prior to that on promotion. So I was having a freak out about how to be in two places at the one time. I am committed to going to Cannes from 12 to 20 May.

FAX FROM Sue to Bruce, 17 March 1994

A catch-up on my fax of yesterday – dictated over the phone from a taxi to our Melinda who incorporated some interesting typos.

Because I'll probably have a whole lot more to report after my visit to Vivian Bullwinkel, etc., on Saturday in Perth, I'm attaching some notes on my conversation with Betty yesterday. I wanted to hug her at the end, she was so warm, direct and honest. She's not terribly well either – hardly surprising at 85. (Although she only looks and acts 75.) I told her we wouldn't be shooting till next year, and she said, 'Oh dear, I hope I can hang on long enough.' She was really sad that she couldn't be there when I meet the others. She and Vivian are very close, I would say.

I guess you thought I'd hit the roof about the dates, but I was worrying all morning, as I went through the *Sirens* campaign plans with Alan Finney, about how I could manage everything.

Thanks for the news about *Sirens*. There's a good buzz here and Roadshow, I have to say, are being really good. They are working their tits off and really enthusiastic and nice.

FAX FROM Sue to Bruce, 22 March 1994

I had a great time in Perth with the girls. I started off at lunch at Cottesloe with Martin Meader, his sidekick Graeme Rattigan (the lawyer) and Herbert and Rose Pinter. Then Martin took me off to Nedlands, to Vivian's house, where Edie Leembruggen who was fourteen when she was imprisoned and eighteen when she was freed, and Cara Kelson were gathered. Cara was not in the camp but went to the Royal Academy of Music in the late 1930s and had somehow connected and corresponded with, although never actually met, Norah Chambers. Also present was Vivian's husband Frank, a dear old soul with a shock of white hair and a friendly smile. We had a smashing afternoon tea and at 6 o'clock Frank said, 'I think we should toast the film with champagne', so out came a bottle of Seaview.

They were terribly friendly and are very excited about the film. Gradually they started to talk. Vivian and about half a dozen nurses went back to Bangka Island only last year to dedicate a memorial to the nurses who died, and she showed me photographs of that. It would have been great to go up there with them.

FAX FROM Sue to Bruce, 28 March 1994

No wonder I haven't heard from you – off skiing again! Life is just fun fun fun for you.

I hate to be a nagger, but I am having lunch the day after tomorrow with Mark Geremia and possibly Greg Coote, and it would be helpful to have an update on whatever is going on in your head (if anything) about *A Voice Cries Out*. Greg always seems to have the latest information (he told me that Sharon Stone was probably not doing the Monroe picture), and apart from that, I don't want to appear at cross purposes with your ideas.

Sirens is now definitely opening here 28 April.

28-MAR 00:33 AM Bruce Beresford Page 1

FAXED

TO BRUCE

28/3/94
Dear Sue,
It isn't all bickies and premieres over here. I've been worki n like a demon trying to finish the cutting on SILENT FALL, a job made complicated by the oddities of Morgan Creek, who keep putt ing my editing staff off and on at whim without consulting me - so Ikeep mysteriously losing sound and music editors just when I needthem. This is all being done in the interests of saving money butis in fact costing a fortune.
Sharon Stone is NOT doing "The Immortals" & I'm sure never had any intention of doing it. However, I'm testing 3 or 4 girls on 5th & 6th April (including Linda Koslowski!). If none of these work out (a strong chance in my view)then I'll take on no other project & just settle down to AVCO. Dino's amazing fee offer has already vanished & I can feel the whole project winding down.
Love,Bruce.

Quel surprise.

Thanks for the info. Sounds good to me.
Herewith letter from one of my new friends. Maybe I should go to see Shelagh Brown after Cannes. Vivian emphasised her too. I think I'll write to her, anyway. Love Sue

Drive time

FILM producer Margaret Fink, who made *My Brilliant Career*, has been ordered off the road for four months after being convicted of drink-driving. Katoomba Court was told last week Ms Fink, 61, said to police: "Haven't you got anything better to do? Why don't you get a proper job." She was also fined $600 on the drink-driving charge and another $200 for making an illegal right hand turn in her black BMW earlier this year at Leura.

FAX FROM Bruce to Sue, 4 April 1994

I've received the book and stuff you sent me – all pretty interesting. We had our second preview last week and should lock in the picture this week. The audience liked the film, which I find a major worry. I'm doing tests for *The Immortals* this Thursday and Friday, but am dubious we'll find anyone.*

Virginia is here and has gone out tonight with John and the lovely Portia [de Rossi], who now speaks with an American accent. I think John could easily get himself a big Hollywood movie with the attention *Sirens* has had, but don't know if this is what he's after.

Extract from the *Australian*
'Film casts around for the "Elusive Oppy"', 8 April 1994

Australian sporting legend, political stalwart and diplomat Sir Hubert Opperman knows just the sort of motivated, romantic young actor who should play him in a major feature film planned for international release.

'We're looking for a handsome young man with a good mop of hair who can ride a bicycle,' the 89-year-old cycling legend said as he joined film producers to announce details of the film in Melbourne yesterday.

Sir Hubert won't be in the film but he and his wife of 66 years, Lady Mavys Opperman, were eager to lend their support yesterday as plans for filming in September moved into top gear. [...]

The first coup by producers has been to secure the services of director Nadia Tass. [...] A lot of international directors showed interest. [...] The Opperman movie – a $10 million production to be financed by a public float – should be in cinemas next April.

---

* *The Immortals* was about the last days of Marilyn Monroe, and her affair with Robert Kennedy. The script was by a Cuban lady whose name I can't remember. The story was a hot potato at the time so the studios were wary of financing it. Subsequently it turned out that the incidents in the script were accurate. BB

Samson Productions Pty Limited
119 Pyrmont Street, Pyrmont, NSW 2009, Australia
Telephone: (02) 660 3244 Facsimile: (02) 692 8926
A.C.N. 000 637 598

13/4/94

12 April 1994

Sue — MARILYN has fallen through. I'll talk to Greg Coote tomorrow re AVCO.
CAN'T CAST IT!
Bruce

TO: BRUCE BERESFORD

Dear Bruce

BLACK ROBE screened on TV here on Sunday night. It was up against Basic Instinct and Indiana Jones III (or whatever). It came second to Basic Instinct everywhere except Perth, where it topped the ratings, peaking at 43! (West Australians prefer art to sex, obviously).

HOORAY!! (What I mean is, hooray for me & the dear old ladies)

I have some more good things to send you re AVCO.

Any news?

Love Sue

Sue Milliken   Tom Jeffrey

SAMSON PRODUCTIONS   ID:61-2-6928926   12 APR '94   16:51 No.019 P.01

FAX FROM Sue to Bruce, 15 April 1994

I guess you are drowning your sorrows after the news about *Marilyn*. It's always a big let down when a picture deflates. I trust you did not misinterpret my exuberance at *our* good fortune as tasteless.

John [Duigan] arrives tomorrow. Roadshow are going all out with the promotion – it's Miramax's (actually our) money, so they're letting themselves go.

FAX FROM Bruce to Sue, 17 April 1994

I'm virtually certain that the *Marilyn* film is dead. We tested five girls but only two of them are real possibilities and the MGM heavy thought one of them (Jeanne Tripplehorn) didn't really look enough like Marilyn, while the other (Melanie Griffith) cannot, he said, remember a line of dialogue under any circumstances. Evidently he's still in therapy over a film he produced with her six years ago.

Dino is now trying Fox and tells me they are 'interested', *but* he told me Sharon Stone was signed for the role when all she'd said was she didn't want to do it. Despite an excellent script I'm now wary of the whole thing, partly because people's image of Marilyn is so definite.

I've spoken to Greg Coote and told him I'll be back in touch this week after the Fox meeting, which I'm sure will come to nothing.

I've finished the picture editing on *Silent Fall*. It might be quite a good film but who wants to see a movie about child abuse? I talked with Greg about going to Singapore early May to meet our mysterious Chinese investor.

Good luck with the Aussie release of *Sirens*. I'm sure it'll do well and get mostly good reviews as it has here. I heard a group of guys discussing it at a lunch place a few days ago – all along the lines of the artist's public responsibility, etc. Not one of them mentioned all the nude models, which surprised me.

FAX FROM Sue to Bruce (written on the above and faxed back)

I have a Dino doll and it's full of pins! I'm going to Cannes 12 May and I'm flat out like a lizard drinking till then. Anyway, I don't trust your promises any more. Let's *ink* the end of May – what about meeting in London and visiting Shelagh Brown and then coming on down?*

FAX FROM Sue to Bruce, 22 April 1994

You are quiet as a mouse – is this good news or bad news? I would like to get a fix on the future – especially what I'm doing early June.

The premiere was a fantastic success. Everyone seemed to really like the film, and we got amazing publicity – front page of the *Australian* and the *Tele/Mirror*, and the arts page of the *SMH*.

* Shelagh Brown and her mother were POWs in the Sumatra camps and Shelagh was a member of the vocal orchestra.

FAX FROM Bruce to Sue, 24 April 1994

I'm now certain that the *Marilyn* film isn't going to happen, although I have a meeting with Dino in the morning. I think he messed it all up by telling everyone he had Sharon Stone when all along she'd insisted she wasn't interested! I'm certain we wasted our time doing the (elaborate) tests with five other actresses as neither MGM nor Fox had the slightest intention of going with any of them. They could've told Dino this instead of letting him spend around $80,000!

I'm pretty fed up with everyone's behaviour over the whole thing. Dino at least has the excuse of being carried away with enthusiasm; he just didn't hear Sharon say 'no'.

I've been offered a lot of scripts but have only glanced at a couple as I've been so busy with the post-synch. Paramount gave me a wonderful script of *Dodsworth*, written by Alfred Uhry, and I met with Harrison Ford about it, but found him totally uncommunicative, even morose, so that one went nowhere.

I had dinner with Greg Coote last night and told him that my plan now is to do the rewrite on *A Voice Cries Out* over the next three months. He was rather vague when I talked about an ideal time to shoot the film, perhaps not surprisingly as he'd no doubt assumed the whole thing would happen after the *Marilyn* film was done. If it's impossible to move the project forward (I'd like to know what you think about this) then I could still do another film beforehand – after finishing off the script, of course. There is one other project, in Europe that could be slotted in late this year. I haven't said anything to them yet, other than I think the script is quite good, and I'm not certain they have all their money. *But* if I tell them I am available things will start moving.

Do we need to contact any 'star' names at a fairly early stage? I mention this only because we'd talked about Judy Davis and I've heard a few extraordinary, and rather worrying, stories lately about her behaviour on set. She is certainly one of the most gifted actresses that have worked in film, so it's hard to understand, as such behaviour is usually the province of the frustrated and untalented.

I remember talking to her a few years ago about *A Passage to India*, directed by the legendary David Lean. One of the English crew said to me 'that Miss Davis didn't like our Mr Lean'. I asked Judy about this and she replied that the film was a mess and Lean didn't have proper control over the material. Despite the acclaim the film had critically I think it is the most ineptly directed of Lean's films and my feeling is he had little sympathy for E. M. Forster's moody and oblique novel. I can understand Judy's frustration but all the same a director with his track record (*Great Expectations* and *Oliver Twist* are two of the best films ever made!) deserves nothing but respect.

Cordelia has had a couple of documentaries on TV in England and is in New York now doing another one. Adam is still teaching Classics but it's impossible to get any information out of him about it.

FAX FROM Bruce to Sue, 25 April 1994

I definitely won't do another film before *A Voice Cries Out* if it's possible to plan as you propose. The only reason I thought it might be possible was if there was no way we could get the film going until late next year. If this isn't the case then I'll work on the script exclusively and then begin the pre-production. I agree with you, it's a major undertaking and needs a lot of time and care.

No, I'm not searching for other 'more exciting things' here. I've told the dreaded Lenny to tell everyone I'm busy and can't consider other projects.

FAX FROM Sue to Bruce, 26 April 1994

Kiss, kiss, kiss – and that's because Chris has just read me your latest fax.

I suppose my main urgency for getting you down here is because I am worried that the dear old girls will die before you get here. If you come in June, it would still mean we could go and see Mr Yap as he will be in Singapore until 30 June.

PS. Is it true that your sister Helen is Elle Macpherson's godmother?*

FAX FROM Sue to Bruce, 26 April 1994

After that long and exceedingly uninteresting message I left on your machine, I remembered there were a couple of other things.

Attached are a couple of clippings. While I can't help feeling irritated at the thought of *A Chance for Glory*, I am nonetheless very happy that we got *A Voice Cries Out*, as it's by far the better project, as far as I'm concerned. I think they'll have a tough time raising ten million bucks from the public after the Hogan fiasco [*Lightning Jack*].

A pity about the Marilyn project but perhaps a blessing – maybe not a great idea to rush into something like that where, as you say, everyone has their own idea of Marilyn, not to mention the Kennedys. If Greg was vague about shooting dates for *A Voice Cries Out*, it was probably because he doesn't have an opinion. I think it's really up to us to decide. I don't think we could start shooting before April or May, climate wise, but that would mean pre-production in February, so given that you will spend three months, or possibly longer, on the rewrite, it doesn't leave much time to shoot another movie.

We really need a good draft to go to actors, and I am keen to do that asap. It could be a quite wonderful ensemble of 'name' women

---

* My sister Helen *is* Elle Macpherson's godmother. BB

actors. I'm still keen on trying to get Emma Thompson, as she would be money in the bank and wonderful as Norah Chambers. She can only say no.

I got a fax this morning which indicates that Mr Yap will be in Singapore from 15 May to 30 June. If you can meet me in London we could fly down to Singapore, and do him on the way to Australia.

Extract from *Variety*
'Aussie Pix Take Stock of Oz Market'

Paul Hogan proved with *Lightning Jack* that it's still possible to fund pictures in Australia by raising money from the public, and now two more Aussie films are taking a similar route.

While the jury is still out on the ultimate fate of *Lightning Jack*, the producers of *Billy's Holiday* and *A Chance for Glory* are soon to issue fund-raising prospectuses. [...]

Cascade Films and Lyons-Sinclair Pictures are seeking to raise $A10 million ($7 million) for *A Chance for Glory*, biopic of Sir Hubert Opperman, Australian world champion cyclist of the 1930s. Filming in Australia and France is slated for September, directed by Nadia Tass (Universal's *Pure luck*) and scripted by Peter Yeldham and David Parker.

FAX FROM Sue to Bruce, 2 May 1994

I am going to visit Shelagh in England on 23 May, and as you won't be there I'll come home the next night. I caught a documentary on ABC on Anzac Day about the fall of Singapore. It has some film of the nurses in Singapore – several of them are recognisable as those who died in the Bangka Island massacre. I'm getting a copy for you.

I sent Betty Jeffrey the Meader Giles script, and spoke to her while I was in Melbourne. She said a lot of it is very silly, and she is making notes for me. She is very anxious to show you some of her treasures when you visit.

Now, The Trip. Tom and I have booked a holiday in Broome from 10 July for a week, and I can't change that. So I dearly want our *AVCO* business out of the way before then.

FAX FROM Bruce to Sue, 3 May 1994

I'm going to England this Sunday for two weeks (they're doing pre-mixes) so if you could move your meeting with Shelagh forward a few days I'll be able to see her with you.

Some new complications. It is possible (by no means definite) that I'll do a film as an alternative to the *Marilyn* one. Relax, as this doesn't mean it'll take up any more time than the *Marilyn* one, and won't affect my doing the *Voice* script beforehand.

I've been offered a number of projects here and two of them are interesting. *Bridges of Madison County* is with Clint Eastwood, with Spielberg producing, and might be foolish to turn down provided I can be convinced that the script might work. I'm certainly dubious about this right now, but have meetings with them this Thursday and Friday. This would shoot September–October (which is actually before the shooting period of the *Marilyn* film) and would be finished fairly early next year.

There is no way I'll do any other project before *Voice* except one of these two, and I'll know by the end of the week. Even Lenny recognises the *Voice* commitment and I've heard him telling people I'll be working in Australia.

Good news about the success of *Sirens*. John is the talk of the town here at the moment and could do almost anything he wanted. His price must've gone up considerably.

May 4 '94 15:25 VRP TEL 3102825311 P. 1

FAXED

TO BRUCE BERESFORD

This is now serious. If you are committed to doing AVCO, PLEASE make some time available!

VILLAGE ROADSHOW PICTURES

May 3, 1994

Roadshow are going to finalise your contract with Jenny this week + pay you the first payment immediately you give a date for commencement of the script.

S.

Ms. Sue Milliken
SAMSON PRODUCTIONS
119 Pyrmont Street
Pyrmont, NSW 2009
AUSTRALIA

Re: ***Andrew Yap Meeting***

Dear Ms. Milliken:

Could you please advise me as to a few dates within the next month when both Mr. Beresford and yourself will be available to meet Andrew Yap in Sydney?

Mr. Yap will be flying to Sydney specifically for this meeting and has asked for a venue suggestion from you.

Thank you for your cooperation. I look forward to hearing from you.

Kind regards,

Kristin

Kristin Parker

:kep
by fax: 011-612-692-8926

VILLAGE ROADSHOW PICTURES (U.S.A.) INC.
2121 Avenue of the Stars, Suite 1590, Los Angeles, California USA 90067
Phone (310) 282-5300, Fax (310) 282-5337

FAX FROM Bruce to Sue, 6 May 1994

I don't know yet about the American film. But I'm going to London this Saturday and will begin work on the script and will be doing nothing else. Promise. I'll have two and a half weeks there.

FAX FROM Sue to Bruce, 27 May 1994

I'm back home with a cold and a bad mood which is compounded by a message that Vivian Bullwinkel will be out of the country (in Bali, if you please) from 18 to 26 June, which kind of buggers that week for visiting Perth. Could you schlep it ahead a few days so that we could get to Vivian early next week? I feel in my bones that this trip is incredibly important. Perhaps it's because one of them might well die at any time (most probably Betty Jeffrey, the best of them all, who is 85 and just had a slight stroke), and because I need that bit of time to talk to you about *A Voice Cries Out* free of the distractions of the hundreds of other things in your life. I just feel if we do this, I can pull the rest of it together, while not impinging too much on the frightful *Bridges of Madison County*.

I spent a day with Shelagh Brown, notes attached. All these women seem to have a special quality – they reach out to you, where most people tend to hold back on first meeting.

FAX FROM Bruce to Sue, 29 May 1994
Los Angeles

Thanks for all the info. I've only been back here since Tuesday (spent three days in Iowa looking for locations for *Bridges*) and have been busy in the mixing theatre all week.

The only problem with the Australian trip is that I've just had a call from Kathy Kennedy [leading Hollywood producer] suggesting we do screen tests with three of the European actresses I've suggested for the movie. This could be late June, but tomorrow I will sort it out for sure.

I'm spending a lot of time here reading all the material for *A Voice Cries Out*. As well as the notes I made in the Imperial War Museum I've done a lot more from the various diaries. All of this points to how incredibly superficial, trivial and corny the current script is and, worst of all, how devoid of characterisation. There is more work than I thought but, on the other hand, I'm more convinced than ever that there is a great film in all this.

Send me the address of the Russian boy who made it to California.

FAX FROM Sue to Bruce, 30 May 1994

Little Mischa's address is below. Apparently they called him Mischa because that was inscribed on his mother's wedding ring. His real name (I guess he was too young to tell them) was Isadore. He must be about our age.

FAX FROM Sue to Greg Coote, Mark Geremia and Kim Vecera, cc Bruce, 1 June 1994

Attached is a copy of a fax to Bruce which sums up today's phone conversations. The bad news is that we will have to give Mr Yap a miss. I can only squeeze a week out of Bruce, and he wants to go straight back to LA. Given the priorities at this stage, I think we must make sure he meets as many of the survivors as possible. Would you like me to write an apology to Mr Yap personally?

In regard to travel, if it's okay with you we will do the internal arrangements through Samson as it's more efficient given the lack of margins in the schedule. We could also do Bruce's international but would you prefer it to go through Roadshow? I think we should travel biz around Australia except for the Perth leg which is punishing enough and should be first class.

Bruce wants to stay in a hotel in Sydney and I'm sure you don't have any objections to that.

FAX FROM Bruce to Sue, 1 June 1994

Sue, the schedule is fine *avec moi*. Bruce.

FAX FROM Sue to Bruce, 9 June 1994

On your Tuesday in Sydney, would you spare an hour to visit my office? The girls work so hard for us and they would love to see you. While you're there we could run through with Chris all the places you have searched for *The Getting of Wisdom* and *Don's Party*. Then I can write to Phillip on behalf of the AFC as the major investor in the films, and ask him to inform us where the negatives are.

I visited Betty Jeffrey on Monday. It was more social than research, because she is in the Heidelberg Repat Hospital. She is very sharp and shows no physical effects of the stroke, but she threw me out after about an hour and a half, as she was getting tired (or maybe just bored, although that is impossible to contemplate).

FAX FROM Bruce to Sue, 1 July 1994

Thanks again for the great organisation which made the trip go so smoothly. It was tremendously interesting to meet the old dears; makes me realise how essential it is now to talk to some of the English and Dutch survivors.

Things are frantic here. I shot tests on film yesterday, for *Bridges*, with Pernilla August, Lena Olin and Sônia Braga and have a lot more people to audition. Warners have even insisted I go to Paris this week (on the way back from Karlovy Vary) to talk to Claudia Cardinale and Catherine Deneuve, although they admit both are too old for the role! Some high-powered agents must have been applying a lot of pressure.

I think August–September would be best to shoot next year, to give me maximum time to get that script right. I can't do what John does and write three or four scripts simultaneously while shooting. I really have to have a period where my mind isn't occupied with anything else. As you know I'm very enthusiastic about the project and wouldn't like to hand it over to anyone else to write. I feel that if we did so, I'd end up totally rewriting it anyway – just as I did with *Mister Johnson* and *The Getting of Wisdom*. At least I'm so far into the research now that an important barrier (sheer knowledge of events) has almost been crossed. The biggest problem is a storyline.

That book of interviews with Japanese soldiers is fabulous. Talk about horrors. You should read the bits where they all become cannibals. A few of them didn't think much of the Australians as jungle fighters!

FAX FROM Sue to Bruce, 4 July 1994

Getting to understand this story is a kind of journey of discovery, and anyone who writes the script has to have taken the trip. The events are not really plot-based, instead the story has to be character-based and deeply insightful. I think it has to be a very emotional (albeit often funny) story. A detached view won't work. Music has to be an integral element and, cleverly used, should help overcome the lack of forward drive. There are so many great musical moments – 'The Captives' Hymn', 'Silent Night' to the men on Christmas Eve, the nuns singing 'Bolero' to Norah as she leaves the camp – this may be one situation where more *is* more (even though a build-up to the orchestra has to be achieved). There are a lot of challenges, in particular the characterisations and relationships of the women, and how to put the Japanese on screen as real people.

I'm sure you'll be as interested as I am to hear that the Oppy movie failed to raise even a fraction of the budget from its prospectus. Oppy was a floppy. In all the writing about it, Ken and Clayton are named as the producers. That, I suspect, was always the problem.

FAX FROM Bruce to Sue, 24 July 1994

I've just returned from London where I shot a *Bridges* scene with eight(!) actresses. Three were fairly absurd choices, forced on me by the studio, but the others were pretty good. I screen the tests for the heavies tomorrow. I know they really want Susan Sarandon so their reactions will be interesting.

I spent a day in Iowa on the way back to check out the renovations on the ruined farmhouse. It's going really well.

All the same, I'm dubious, to say the least, of this film going ahead with me at the helm. It is so high profile that everyone is getting involved in decisions that should really be mine, or mostly mine. I'm becoming increasingly afraid that I'll never be able to do the movie I'm convinced should be done from this book. I haven't signed my contract and have warned Lenny I might bail out at the end of this week – in which case I'll go to France, as planned, and get going on the script for *A Voice Cries Out.*

I don't think this action will cause any problems with Warners as Spielberg and I have clashed so much over the script (he's a nice guy and is actually trying to be helpful!) that they'll be glad to see the last of me. Their reaction is invariably 'just do what Steven says' – and it's hard to argue against this when you're dealing with far and away the most successful director of all time. I'll keep you posted. I actually *want* to make the film and think it could be a winner, but can't afford to be backed into a position where I'm making the wrong movie.

Meanwhile I've read more and more on the prison camps and have made copious notes. I saw the *Tenko* episodes [1980s TV series]. It's really just a soap opera in an unusual setting and I didn't see anything there worth pinching.

I wrote to all the ladies we met, from Karlovy Vary. It was very worthwhile meeting them.

FAX FROM Sue to Bruce, 26 July 1994

Thanks for your most interesting and rather startling fax. Naturally being a decent and fair-minded person I do hope the problems resolve themselves. On *the other hand...*

I wrote on spec to Elizabeth Simons in Tasmania to see if she would cough up any more gritty information, but got a polite no.

I had a very uninteresting 25 minutes with Greg Coote last week, in which he told me all the fab projects Village Roadshow are planning (*Kangaroo Kid* and *The Fatal Shore* – have I heard all this before?), told a funny story then moved on to his next meeting. Mark Geremia has been on the phone, having a bit of a moan about when are you going to write the script, so I told him to just be patient and not worry. What choice has he got?

I've just finished reading *By Eastern Windows* written by an American journalist who was locked up in the Men's Camp. It's interesting to compare the account of how the men coped as opposed to the women. They seemed to mix much more across Dutch and British lines, and to squabble amongst themselves far more.

The author mentions a man called Harrison, who was I think Deputy Chief Engineer of the Malayan railways. I suppose it's too long a coincidence to think that this might be Rhoisin's father. He comes out of it rather well.*

We had a great week in Broome. Such a beautiful place. Much of the architecture is a mixture of oriental and Australian colonial, and many of the new buildings are constructed of corrugated iron like the old pearling houses and factories, which is very pleasing on the eye. The Cable Beach Club is probably the best-designed resort I've seen. It's entirely built out of corrugated iron, inside and out, and the exterior colours are dark green and that bright Chinese

---

* This was indeed the father of Bruce's first wife, Rhoisin.

lacquer-red. Inside it is cool white with dark polished wood. Palms and silver gums and flowers around lots of streams and pools keep the buildings separate and private. The food is okay but the service is definitely Broome-time and it's wise not to want anything in a hurry.

The *Bran Nue Dae* boys drove us to an Aboriginal settlement called Lombadina about 200 km from Broome and we stayed at a rustic little resort with cabins built of paperbark overlooking the sea, with a remarkably good restaurant. After dinner the boys got out their guitars and played and sang songs from the musical, on the restaurant terrace under the stars.

The old mission church at Lombadina reminded me of the church in the Huron village in *Black Robe* – so much so that I wonder if Herbert didn't get his inspiration from the Australian one. The landscape is dazzling with the reddest, red ochre of the Australian desert coming right down to a turquoise and cobalt sea.

I got on fine with Jimmy Chi and the boys, who have asked me to produce the movie. I've agreed subject to settling acceptable terms. It will be filmed as a road movie travelling from Perth to Lombadina via the Pinnacles, the dolphins at Monkey Mia and Broome. With the energy of the piece, the music and the landscape, I think it has the potential to be really something.*

In other news, Sheila Helpmann died – 78. I remember her in *The Getting of Wisdom*, and I worked with her myself once, on an episode of *Boney* [1970s TV series].

Sirens has opened well in London, with quite good reviews and excellent opening week box office. John has been nominated for an

---

* In spite of government funding agency support and five years' work, during which I sent *Bran Nue Dae* to over 50 sales agents/distributors, I could get no commercial backing. Nearly fifteen years later Robyn Kershaw and Rachel Perkins raised the money and made the film, which was a considerable hit.

AWGIE for his script but I think *Muriel's Wedding* will win. We are going to Melbourne for the AWGIES, then skiing for a few days with friends of Tom's at Falls Creek. Bliss.

I'll be waiting with intense curiosity for more news about *Bridges*. What a dilemma. Spielberg is the master of the Mills & Boon approach, which goes gangbusters with this material. I think Susan Sarandon would be good as the woman. Her empathy would overcome the slight credibility problem of her playing an Italian. With so many other credibility problems with the story, who'd be worrying? I read the other day that the book continues to top the bestseller list in the US. Extraordinary. There must be a lot of women out there looking at their husbands and thinking, 'Oh God, just give me Clint Eastwood for the weekend.'

FAX FROM Bruce to Sue, 2 August 1994

It's only quiet here because there's been nothing much to say. I'm still not doing *Bridges*, so we've been packing up here (LA) and go back to London on Saturday. We plan to rent a place in France or Italy for the rest of the summer and I'll continue on the script of *A Voice Cries Out*.

I called Helen Colijn today and left a message.* If she's around I'll go up to San Francisco and see her on Friday.

FAX FROM Sue to Bruce, 4 August 1994

After our conversation this morning I spoke to Mark Geremia as Greg Coote had left for the day. We discussed the financing program for the film, and he agreed that it will take a lot less than six months to pull the money together from the moment we have a script. It only

---

* Helen, a young Dutch woman in the camps, was instrumental in reviving the vocal orchestra music in the 1980s and wrote a book about her experiences, *Song of Survival*.

took me six months to finance *Sirens* from a standing start! This will be a *lot* easier, with Andrew Yap's money and you attached.

Mark is going to speak to Greg about it tomorrow, and try to work out a timetable that will work for you and Lenny. My concern is that if you take another film it will blow the possibility of shooting next year. So you might just have to do some commercials between drafts.

Anyway, I'm at least pleased that you are able to go to work on the script. I appreciate the difficulty about the narrative line, which is why the characterisation is going to be so important. Dramatically the story has the advantage that all the heroines survive with the exception of Margaret Dryburgh, whose death with Norah singing the Twenty-Third Psalm to her should have the cinema in floods.

FAX FROM Bruce to Sue, 8 August 1994

I saw Helen Colijn on Friday. It was most useful to have a Dutch point of view on the events in the camp. Helen's recall was excellent and she told me one quite amazing story. She and her sisters actually met their father by the fence one day – after he'd slipped away from a work party – and he gave them a chicken for Christmas. They never saw him again; he died shortly before the war ended.

It's announced in the paper today that Jessica Lange is doing *Bridges* and Clint is directing. Jessica was the one they wanted me to use in the first place. I resisted (pointlessly) as I think she is talented but cold (fatal to the role) and would make an unconvincing Italian.

FAX FROM Sue to Bruce, 11 August 1994

I'm glad it went well with Helen Colijn. I have just finished reading *Six Bells off Java* and there is a riveting account of her shipwreck and lifeboat trip to Sumatra. She fell in love with a young ship's officer; they spent most of what must have been a ghastly journey in the back of the lifeboat cooing at each other. They planned to marry when they got to Sumatra, but the Japs got to them first.

I had breakfast with the new head of acquisitions at Samuel Goldwyn, Ronna Wallace, on Sunday and she is dead keen on *A Voice Cries Out* – and on you. I told her the budget and she didn't flicker. I promised them a script when it's done. She asked how you felt about Goldwyn's handling of *Black Robe* and I said not too thrilled. Everyone has changed there now.

We completely missed out on AFI Award nominations for *Sirens* – only got best actress, music and sound. A big insult to John. Perceptions about *Sirens* are excellent outside Australia and the woman from Goldwyn's was raving about its success.

I'm glad there is nothing else tempting you at the moment. I've got a little Lenny doll and I've locked it in a dark cupboard.

FAX FROM Bruce to Sue, 11 August 1994

I received the tape by Ned Lander. He's made a really fascinating documentary, which I've found very helpful.*

I saw *Blackfellas* today too. It's a terrific film. Obviously made on a very low budget but done with a lot of commitment. The Aboriginal actor [David Ngoombujarra] in the co-lead is quite outstanding. Know anything about him?

Barry Humphries is doing a show in provincial Denmark!

You must also see the French comedy *Les Visiteurs*. Also the Italian realist thriller *La Scorta*.

FAX FROM Sue to Bruce, 12 August 1994

I've just come from seeing Greg Coote. Boy, what a name-dropper! Anyway, he said he spoke to Tom Rothman this morning (now at Fox Classics) and he thinks it's likely they will put up the money to

---

* *Fifty Years of Silence* is about Ned's then mother-in-law, Jan Ruff O'Herne's experience as a comfort woman in Java in WWII.

do the whole thing, if that's what we want. So Fox, Goldwyn and Miramax all want it. I think it's looking very good, particularly as Roadshow (being so rich) have the ability to cashflow distribution deals.

We did the completion guarantee on *Blackfellas*. The director isn't one of my favourites but it's a surprisingly good film. David won an AFI award for his performance. He hadn't done much before, or since, due to the few roles for Aborigines. Such a shame, as he is very talented.

I'm glad you found *Fifty Years of Silence* interesting. Wasn't she brave?

I've heard of out-of-town tryouts, but Barry's show in Denmark beats everything.

I hope you all enjoy the time in France. I think I'll take a couple of weeks off and just stay home and read books. I'm pretty tired. Chris will always know where I am.

Extract from *The Hollywood Reporter*, 'Streep takes *Bridges* leap', 15 August 1994

In a move that took Hollywood by surprise, Meryl Streep has been cast opposite Clint Eastwood in *The Bridges of Madison County*... The studio on Friday also confirmed that Eastwood would replace Bruce Beresford as director on the project... A primary reason Beresford left the project was the studio's desire to cast an American female lead, while Beresford remained fixed on a European actress. Streep, who is known for her ability to cover foreign accents, represents the best of both worlds.

FAX FROM Bruce to Sue, 27 August 1994

Well I *am* actually working away and finding it very difficult too. I went through the Meader Giles draft very carefully, and find it's even less helpful than I had thought. Their main character is practically the German doctor and the sympathetic portrayal of her would arouse the wrath of every survivor – not one of whom had a good word to say about her!

I'm going to do *Last Dance* for Disney – a script I'd agreed to *before* the *Bridges* shambles. We shoot early January and I start pre-production 10 October. I fervently hope to have the script by then.

I have a *suitcase* of reference stuff with me and almost no clothes. We see Dino De Laurentiis tonight and Jeff Smart tomorrow night so social life continues.

FAX FROM Sue to Bruce, 29 August 1994

I always knew you would have to throw that script away and start again. I hope you can pull it off.

What does *Last Dance* do to *Voice*? Please let me know if it cancels any prospect of doing *Voice* next year. I've no doubt we can finance it very quickly once the script is showable, but I don't want anyone under false impressions – least of all me! But it does sound as though the timing won't work.

FAX FROM Bruce to Sue, 30 August 1994

I'll contact Sylvia Cartner when I'm back in London.

I don't know if Veronica Turner's diary would add a lot. I find the women very circumspect in comparison to the men (in prison camps). *By Eastern Windows* is much more forthright than anything by any of the ladies. Still, if we can afford it you might as well have the photocopying done.

The Disney film should be all done by end of July. We could start later in the year. Keep your fingers crossed over this script – I find the women's reticence creates a problem for me – it'd be far easier to film *By Eastern Windows* or G. F. Jacobs' book *Prelude to the Monsoon*, which are full of conflicts and characters. But I'm blasting on.

I hear Cecil Holmes died. Poor old bloke. Hope he got some decent obits. A great shame he never managed to make a few films in the early 1970s when everyone was doing it. Can't imagine how he missed out.

LETTER TO Sue from Helen Colijn, 3 September 1994

It was great meeting you on the phone three days ago. As discussed I am sending you the manuscript of *Song of Survival: Women Interned.*

The Way of a Boy is a little gem. The book points up the conflicts all camp mothers had, many thousands of them all over the Japanese camps, in raising their children. How to explain that it is a sin to steal from each other, but okay, even heroic, to steal from the enemy? 'It is hard to stay alive, but even harder to stay alive and decent,' says the author's mother. And how do you explain to a child that one should love the enemy?

Kindest regards, also to Chris Gordon.

FAX FROM Sue to Bruce, 12 September 1994

How's the oeuvre? (Not an oeuf, I hope).

I am back in the office after three weeks, the last two at home.

One of the things I did was to read *Three Came Home*. Because she's such a good writer, it really pulls it all together, doesn't it? She's very frank, too, particularly for the time when she wrote it. It's terrifically moving and insightful. Obviously the Japanese had a master plan for treating prisoners, as the experience seems to have been much the same in all the islands. Thanks to you kindly suggesting to Helen Colijn that I might know about publishers for *her* book in Australia, she is sending me a copy. I'm keen to read it, but the chances of getting it published here have to be zero.

Spring is here it seems, epitomised by a kite festival at Bondi yesterday. What a sight! At least a hundred, maybe more, kites floating over Bondi beach – huge ones competing for prizes, little ones flown by kids. Every colour you could think of. Octopuses, dragons, eagles, snakes. Against a perfect blue sky and white sand, and board riders hanging languidly off waves in the warm sunshine. Thousands of people, many children, mums helping to get kites untangled and into the air. A nice stiff breeze tempering the sunshine and taking the kites up, up.

I heard on the radio this morning that Jessica Tandy died. I guess you'll be pretty sad. It said ovarian cancer. Creepy that it can kill you even at 85.

FAX FROM Bruce to Sue, 12 September 1994

How sad about Jessica – a shame you never met her; a really great person.

I am still working away. It's quite a struggle as I'm finding the characters and plot line very tough. I think this first draft will be fairly rough – by the way, I've started it in Singapore as I feel it's essential to show life there as a contrast to the camp.

Three Came Home is excellent, *n'est-ce pas*? But we can't film that – it's already been done! *By Eastern Windows* is also first class.

FAX FROM Bruce to Sue, 18 September 1994

Frank Gare called me yesterday to say that Nene died *last May.** I had no idea and guess you didn't either. You must have been out of Australia when the obituaries were in the papers. Remember I phoned them a number of times when we were in Perth? There was

---

* Nene Gare, the author of *The Fringe Dwellers* and several other novels, had become a friend during the making of the film.

no answer but it seems that Frank just happened to be out when I called. Evidently Nene has another book coming out next year. She was pretty wonderful – not just talented but warm and kind.

I continue to struggle with the script.

FAX FROM Sue to Bruce, 19 September 1994

Thanks for your fax about Nene. It was followed by a phone call from Frank, and we had a long chat which had me very close to tears. How sad! It was awful, too, because I was so sure she was still alive. I had even seen her on TV only a couple of weeks ago – a very brief interview in a documentary, but no indication that she had died. It must have been while I was in Cannes, because I neither heard nor saw a word. Frank is going to send me the obituaries, and I'm doing a tape of *Fringe Dwellers* for his daughter.

Helen Colijn's book is curiously readable because it's from the heart, although not terribly well written. It gives yet another facet of the story, and she is fairly frank about the less than loveable ones. She seems to have excised the lifeboat romance very thoroughly. It occurred to me after reading it that the very ordinary lives that became so extraordinary for that period is one of the really interesting things about the story. If you are starting it in Singapore maybe you should go even further and start with a group of old ladies. I've seen photographs and film of the nurse survivors attending a dedication ceremony at Duntroon a few years ago – when they were haler than they are now. They are all extremely well dressed, with big colourful hats, a vibrant bunch; if you didn't know they could just as easily be the bowling club's women's committee. To see them gathering in the morning for breakfast at a hotel like the one we stayed at in Canberra, all chatting and dithering around together, then very dignified at the Duntroon ceremony in the winter sunshine, then back to Singapore… it would shorten the time you had to devote to the camps, and might lend itself to a voice over, to help the story along.

FAX FROM Sue to Bruce, 22 September 1994

I've just finished reading [Sister] Veronica Clancy's diary – it's another good read, probably as well written as Helen Colijn's book. It's in a slight mess as the manuscript typed by her brother has been deposited in the Australian War Memorial with a few pages missing and some odd photocopying. But the whole story is there, and she is quite outspoken at times. She makes no bones about Dr G!

I also particularly liked the moment in Helen's book where the Australian nurses all turn up for the first vocal orchestra concert all wearing the same loud orange lipstick. It could be a very funny moment.

PS. I've been invited to cocktails with the new Consul-General of Japan!

FAX FROM Bruce to Sue, 22 September 1994

Thanks for the note with the info about Veronica Clancy's diary – and the extract.

I have to be very careful with the portrayal of Dr G. I am not glamorising her but it won't look very PC if I have a camp with all these well-bred English ladies and gutsy Aussie nurses, while a major turd is the Jewish doctor. Jews are, of course, no more or less estimable than anyone else and if Dr G was as ghastly as they say, then they were just unlucky, *but*, in the film, because of the selective framework, it's going to look like a pointed comment. Also, it could be extremely tasteless given the suffering of Jews in the German camps.

I am staggering on and have absolutely no idea whatever what it's all like. I've spent the last few days revising the first 50 pages. Structure is a major problem as it's essential to set up heavy-duty suffering in order for the choir to be effective. I also found I needed the Singapore opening for contrast; somehow just having them washed up on the shores of Sumatra didn't seem enough. Using the current batch of old ladies isn't a bad idea in a way but was done in *Schindler's List*. I'll try to think of a variation on it.

I'm using fictitious names (though this could be changed) because I've really had to make composite characters. If we identify people specifically it ties me down to certain patterns of behaviour, is restrictive, and could easily have everyone up in arms at the slightest variation from their perception of themselves.

FAX FROM Sue to Bruce, 23 September 1994

I take your point about Dr G, and I had been wondering if we need to identify her as Jewish. I think what got her in the clink was her British passport (which Veronica says she produced when the Allies won the war). If she had a name, which was not identifiably Jewish and it was never mentioned we might get away with it. I do agree you have to be careful, it could look very unbalanced, with the wisdom of hindsight. Basically she was a bitch and a collaborator and could have been any nationality, but being German gave her an in with the Japs. But there were at least a couple of other doctors in the camp who were saints, etc. So the Goldberg character is basically a bit of sand in the oyster. (Well, not much of an oyster.)

I think the anti-Semitism was part of the overall racist attitudes of the time. They're the attitudes of the 1930s, without benefit of the dreadful events during the war, and basically the white European middle class considered themselves superior to pretty well everyone. Veronica writes about the native peoples and how wrong it is for them to breed with the whites – 'the results are not wanted by either side'. And they probably weren't in those days. She is quite intolerant of the Eurasians in the camp and says fortunately some Eurasian women who liked 'that sort of thing' took care of the Japanese. On the other hand I think the women would help anyone in need, and their actions were quite a different thing to the way they thought.

I wasn't really thinking of using the current batch of old ladies because I think they'll be far too frail by then. More making-up our characters as 70-year-olds (or finding likely doubles). I think *Schindler's* did it at the end, with real people, and I had quite a different thing in mind. But I guess the point is somewhat the same.

Although I was keen on real names in the beginning, I agree it would present difficulties as you must composite to get all the bits in, and they would probably throw a fit.

FAX FROM Bruce to Sue, 5 October 1994

I've completed a draft and have spent the last few days doing notes for *extensive* revisions. I've no idea whatever what it's like.

I'm scheduled to go to America on 16 October, so am labouring to get the draft to you before that date.

We won't be in Oz this Christmas. Instead we're going to Jamaica where Kathy Shaw is getting married.

FAX FROM Sue to Bruce, 7 October 1994

Good news! (I hope.) Do you mean you are doing the *extensive* revisions now, before you put it in the post? Do you think it's good enough to show people? Guess you don't know if you don't know what it's like. What I want to do, if it is, is to put pressure on Roadshow to go pay or play with you so we can lock in a plan. This would mean getting a pretty good indication of intent from a distributor. But I think that's possible.

I was put right off *Guests of the Emperor* [TV movie] early on when all those women in freshly ironed dresses, hair and make-up perfect, were standing under a palm tree saying we've been shipwrecked. The incompetence of the leadership in Singapore was unbelievable. I've been trying to imagine how I'd behave if bombs were falling in Bondi Road and the government was saying 'Don't worry, everything's fine'.

We saw the Bangarra Dance Company last night – Aboriginal modern dance. Just fantastic. There's some amazing talent coming through in the Aboriginal community.

We'll miss you at Christmas but Jamaica sounds like fun.

Looking forward to getting the script.

FAX FROM Sue to Bruce, 11 October 1994

I am actually surprised you've had so much trouble with the women's stories, you just have to read between the lines a bit more. The men's stories are not *that* much more intimate. I think it's just that you are more comfortable with men bonding rather than women.

We are having a terrible drought here. The weather is really weird. An awful wind has been blowing for weeks, setting off bushfires up and down the coast. One day we're sweltering in the heat and the next we have sweaters on. You have picked a good year to give Christmas in Oz a miss.

Do you think you'll be able to fit in another pass on *Voice* during pre on the Disney movie? Or will it have to wait till 1997? Rhetorical question at this stage.

FAX FROM Bruce to Sue, 11 October 1994

Yes, I am labouring to send the draft to you this weekend, before I fly off to LA! I've really no idea what it's like.

I'll have to do a revision, provided we think there's something there worth revising, but will need some weeks away from it before I can tackle it again.

FAX FROM Bruce to Sue, 12 October 1994

Could be a slightly disastrous set-back. I couldn't get into my file on the computer this morning to finalise the script revisions, it wouldn't open. I found out that there is a limit to the number of pages in each file! And, according to the program people, there is *no way* of getting into the file. I have someone working on it all the same but he doesn't seem too hopeful. If we can't get in there you won't have the draft next week as I have no backup and no printout! All I have is the very first draft printed and it's been so extensively revised that it's quite useless. It means I'll have to do *all* the revisions (a major rewrite) again, which is at least two weeks' work. I might be able to do this (ugh – what a job) after my two to three weeks in US. *If* we do get into the file I'll just have to knuckle down and send it all off to you next Monday.

FAX FROM Sue to Bruce, 13 October 1994

A likely story! Sounds like 'the dog ate my homework'. *Everyone* backs up or prints out as they go. I hope you are composing a fax (handwritten) to Disney at this moment explaining why you won't be arriving till you've done the rewriting.

By a nice little irony there was a message on the answer machine from Ronna Wallace at Goldwyn's this morning asking me to send her the script! I'm not quite sure how to answer… perhaps I'll just wait and not think about it.

Hope you can work a miracle.

FAX FROM Bruce to Sue, 13 October 1994

After working all day the computer guy here has managed to get me a printout of sorts – it crams the 113-page script into 23 pages and would have to be retyped carefully. A tricky job, but at least I haven't lost everything. He's trying one more thing tomorrow to try and retrieve the file in a more accessible form. If he does so I should be able to post the script to Australia on Monday.

FAX FROM Sue to Bruce, 14 October 1994

Well, *that's* a relief, at least of sorts. It must be quite a sight! Chris suggests that you fax us the 23 pages and she will have a go at retyping it here. She's about the best person for such a job and she is very familiar with the story. That way we'd also have it on our disk (with backup, say no more). I can imagine how relieved you are, me only slightly less so.

Since you mentioned titles on the phone I've been thinking about it. The best 'feeling' for the story that I have found is the quote I sent you – *Music, when soft voices die/Vibrates in the memory.* But it's not easy to extract a title from it. I think that the Deathbird idea is probably going the wrong way, as the story is about how the women used music to transcend death. Maybe *The Nightbird*? It would be good if we could find a phrase which indicates hope. I have been cruising through poetry and no doubt you have done this also. Herewith a few ideas:

> *Soft Voices*
> *Women's Song*
> *Miss Dryburgh's Orchestra*

Personally, I like *Nuns in Jeopardy.*

10/14/1994 13:47 0713706916 BERESFORD PAGE 01

Sue, You could start typing This up.
Bruce

TBWPOct 11, 199410:42 am $7é[ÇeÇ!glê/+Çé é#A- 6s ; 7

[illegible]

To BRUCE

VERY FUNNY

FAX FROM Bruce to Sue, 16 October 1994

Sue – Trish is now retyping. I'll Fedex it from CA in one and a half weeks. Sorry.

FAX FROM Sue to Bruce, undated

Lucky Trish! Chris is clapping her hands.

Better late than never is all I can say.

Enjoy five days of Botticelli.

Extract from the *Hollywood Reporter* 'Beresford Joins *The Playmaker*', undated

Bruce Beresford has teamed up with producers Ismail Merchant and James Ivory on *The Playmaker* for Buena Vista. The film will be based on the book by Thomas Keneally. *The Playmaker* will be directed by Beresford, who is currently writing the script with Timberlake Wertenbaker. [... It] is the fact-based story of a band of eighteenth-century convicts who put on Australia's first stage play. Beresford is currently slated to direct *The Last Dance* at Hollywood Pictures and then will jump to shoot his pet project, Village Roadshow's *A Voice Cries Out*.

FAX FROM Sue to Bruce, 23 October 1994

I just had a call from Cara Kelson in Perth to say that Vivian Bullwinkel had a stroke about ten days ago, and is paralysed down her right side. Cara seemed to think full recovery is unlikely, but I guess they can never tell.

I've written to her, and told her the script is currently being unscrambled.

FAX FROM Bruce to Sue, 1 November 1994

I now have Trish's retyped version of the script and am making the amendments I'd already noted down when the computer crashed. Very nice of the *SMH* to note the bad reviews of my film. Did they do the same for Fred [Schepisi] on *Mr. Baseball*? And Peter [Weir] on *Fearless*? Why am I singled out!

Very sorry to hear about poor old Viv.

FAX FROM Sue to Bruce, 16 November 1994

I'm going up to Brisbane next Tuesday and have arranged to visit Nell van de Graaff (*We Survived*). She lives on the Gold Coast and has been asking me to visit her. I just spoke to her on the phone and she sounds very nice and totally together. (Anyone who brought five children through a Japanese POW camp would not be bothered by a little thing like old age.)

The script hasn't arrived yet but I imagine it will turn up by the end of the week.

I had lunch with Aden Young yesterday. He's more beautiful than ever and I love being seen with him at the Bayswater Brasserie. He applied for the directing course at AFTRS and they rejected him without even an interview. In spite of a letter from me! And in spite of him having worked many times at the school in student productions for almost no money. It seemed cruel and tactless not even to give him an interview. He is very keen to write and direct.

FAX FROM Bruce to Sue, 22 November 1994

I'm in London till 4 or 5 December. Anxious to know your reaction to the script. I'll be doing work here on a second draft – provided we all think it's worthwhile. Overall I must say I'm quite pleased, but am sure I'm the worst judge.

FAX FROM Sue to Bruce, 23 November 1994

I got your fax this morning, and wonder if you missed the two notes I sent to London saying that I was visiting Nell van de Graaff, and that I had received the script? I read it the night it arrived, then I went to Brisbane. It's *not bad*. I will make notes but the story is there and it flows, it's interesting and moving. The opening is terrific – Singapore and especially the bombing of the ship. A touch expensive to do (as in Atlanta burns) but great to sell the script. I'm glad you feel good about it because it's a great start.

I'll do some notes before the weekend. I'm going to Broome for a couple of days from Sunday to see the boys.

I had a lovely time with Nell yesterday. All those women are so fantastic – it does seem that the experience weeded out the good ones. She gave me a little book called *Crosses and Tigers* written by a Japanese interpreter on the Burma railway. I'll copy it for you.

FAX FROM Sue to Bruce, 24 November 1994

I just spoke to Greg Coote, who I found at Sydney airport about to board a plane for LA. He has received the script, hasn't read it, plans to do so on the flight. I think it only caught up with him in the last day or so. I did a small rave over it and his response was fascinating. A spontaneous intake of breath, then he said softly, 'That's *fantastic*.' For a moment he wasn't Mr Cool of Beverly Hills. He was *excited*. So I would think you'll hear from him over the weekend. I told him he'd find it a bit expensive but not to worry about it, and he was fine about that. I hope he agrees with us! I told him Lenny loved it – that lets him know it's okay for him to love it too.

Vivian is still in hospital (seven weeks), still can't talk much except yes and no, is very weak but not paralysed on her right side. The physios are working on her and it's hoped she'll be able to go home soon. I'll write to Betty too – and let her read a copy if she wishes.

From a quick but intensive examination it would appear that the script is extremely well constructed. There is so much research material that there are probably some very good moments which merit inclusion. Probably the most important omission is 'The Captives' Hymn'. Not having any music till page 90 is a bit of a handicap, but I think it's a critical inclusion.

Shooting the camps in sequence is a great idea, I'll put a dietician in the budget. So much of it needs the atmospherics of Asia, and the continuity cost of carting people from one country to another might well outweigh any benefit of shooting in Australia. (We don't need to tell Greg this just yet.) But these questions will be answered by a swing through Sumatra, Singapore and Far North Queensland. When might we fit this into your busy schedule?

Basically, it was worth the wait.

FAX FROM Bruce to Sue, 25 November 1994

We are just off to Paris for the weekend. I just switched on the TV and saw a review of *A Good Man in Africa*. The reviewer held up a blackboard at the end of his assessment (assassination) and gave it 1 out of 10! I don't think it deserves any more. I knew when I was directing it that it couldn't possibly work. For some odd reason the script read well but couldn't be made to play, I think because it actually had no coherent story and no detail to the characterisations. The novel is the same but it's stylishly written and it doesn't matter. Boyd's comic novels are as hard to film as Evelyn Waugh's – which have never been done successfully; *A Handful of Dust,* for example, is not even apparently meant to be funny in the film version.

Anyway, on to *The Captives*. I haven't heard from Greg Coote yet.

Thanks for your notes. Many of them are useful and I'll incorporate them in my revision next week.

I had forgotten about that book *Captives* when I thought of the title, at least consciously. I'm not sure if we legally need to do anything to be able to use the title, as I don't believe you can copyright a title. Shortly after I did *Tender Mercies* I found a book of that name. There was also a film made in 1972 called *Captives*, but not *The Captives*.

FAX FROM Sue to Bruce, 28 November 1994
Cable Beach Club, Broome

Another thought: Miss Dryburgh used to say, when it got too much for someone, 'Look up' – meaning the sky, not God. We could do a nice effect shot of a tropical night sky.

More may follow, as and when.

The weather here is rather as our girls might have experienced it.

FAX FROM Sue to Bruce, 1 December 1994

I'm back in Sydney.

I was indeed sorry to hear of the rude reviewer who gave *A Good Man in Africa* 1 out of 10! UIP have the movie here so I'm hoping to get a screening soon. I do think the script was part of your problem – then not helped by the crises during production. I know you won't take any notice of me but (like my Aunt Jenny who used to interfere with the words: 'It's none of my business but I'm *just saying…*') have you thought of *slowing down*, just for a bit? *The Captives* needs a lot of your time and thought, and if you would *spend the time necessary*, I've no doubt you would make a truly wonderful film.

Speaking of which, I caught up with Greg Coote today. He likes the script a lot, found it a good read, had a couple of comments: he was surprised and a little disappointed that there was so little music, and that it came in so late. I explained why but he – and, I expect, most other people – was under the belief that the music would be a much greater feature of the film. I think this will come up again and while I recognise that the solution is not just the obvious one I do think you should try to give more satisfaction through music in the film.

I told him that you are doing a revision this week.

I had a letter from Martin Meader today telling me about Vivian's stroke and asking if I had read *Prelude to the Monsoon*. He tells me now that he knows 'very well' the son of Sgt Gillam who was with Jake Jacobs when the camp was liberated. Funny that he never mentioned it when we were in Perth.

Only one thought has occurred to me since, which is whether the passing of time is clear enough. It may well be, I recall one Christmas and it's probably dealt with adequately elsewhere.

I thought what I'd do with Greg Coote is let him see the revised script and then plot a timetable/financing strategy. I should probably get a budget done on that script also, to give us a ballpark. You didn't respond to my query about when you might fit in a trip to Singapore and Sumatra – May?

I'm feeling a bit spacey as I flew home from Broome via Karratha, Perth and Melbourne – eleven hours and three changes of aircraft! It took all night and is not recommended.*

FAX FROM Bruce to Sue, 1 December 1994

I'm glad to hear that Greg likes the script. I can see room for lots of improvements, but overall I'm quite proud of it and think it could make a wonderfully exciting film.

The fact that the music comes in quite late is deliberate. In my earlier versions (unread by anyone except me) it came in earlier *but* I realised that this was ineffective as there hadn't been enough suffering to make it a response to the prevailing conditions. It was just a bunch of ladies having a sing song. So I rewrote, piling on the ghastly conditions and incidents, so that now when they sing it's much more of a triumph, as well as a statement of defiance. The music will be quite a lot of screen

---

* This was in the middle of the pilots' strike of 1994. SM

time. It's difficult to write more than 'they sing the Dvořák *Largo*' in the script! The vocal sections will be striking aurally and visually, but on paper can't really mean much. No words can convey the glory of Dvořák, Mendelssohn or Elgar.

I think that Susan Macarthy really is the central character but I've created a number of other major roles. Again, in my earlier drafts I had less people but on rereading there never seemed to be enough characters around and the sense of them being all locked up together was absent. I'm now fond of all the people in the story and they're very clear in my mind. I've worked so closely with them for so long it's as if I actually know them. Bett, who I adore, snuck into the script almost by herself; in my original draft she had only one line of dialogue.

I'm inclined to think the passing of time is fairly clear in the script, you'll see I've thrown in a Christmas, plus reference here and there to how long they've been locked up. But I can do a bit more.

I'm going to the US this Sunday for some location finding and casting on *Last Dance*. We're going to Jamaica for the holidays. I could do a Singapore/Sumatra trip in May.

I agree I should slow up a bit, although I'm still very youthful and sprightly. I think it's just that I have constant visions of my supremely lazy father and am still determined not to be like him.

However I am supposed to be directing an opera in America from 6 January to 10 February 1996. This is absolutely my only commitment. I have a Merchant Ivory project but have told them it will have to wait. I am passionately keen to make *The Captives* and have cleared the decks of everything else in order to be able to do so.

FAX FROM Sue to Bruce, 2 December 1994

It might help if you could tell me what you would consider to be the ideal timetable for *Captives* vis-a-vis the Disney flick and the opera. (Include a week's skiing after the opera.) It would then give us something to work towards.

I've just remembered what Nell van de Graaff's retirement village apartment reminded me of – Edie Leembruggen's flat in Perth. It felt very familiar, the Malaysian experience. Not quite as over the top as Edie's but that same fondness for murky brown oriental/islander art and artifacts.

PS. I've suggested to Greg that I come over for a meeting the week you're in LA – don't expect he'll buy it though.

FAX FROM Bruce to Sue, 2 December 1994

I think *Last Dance* should be over by the end of August, so we could begin pre-production, which I agree needs to be done very carefully. I could theoretically still get out of doing the opera but the company will throw a fit and it probably isn't necessary anyway as the shooting could begin in May or June 1996. If this is truly impossible for some reason or other and I have to cancel directing the opera I should know asap. I'm actually casting the main roles for it in New York on 10 and 11 December! At least with the opera we know exactly what's involved and it can't drag on like a film. Rehearsal is exactly four to five weeks and then it's performed for four nights and that's that.

FAX FROM Bruce to Sue, 6 December 1994

I haven't finished the revisions due to work on *Last Dance* and the opera, but will have time next week. I've not heard from Greg Coote – odd considering he faxes me every time he rolls over in bed. I think the current script is good enough to gauge anyone's interest.

I've just read a funny and touching Aussie novel by Madeleine St John (also at uni with me) and think we should buy it. *Please read it* and give me your opinion. It's short, called *The Women in Black*. About ladies working at David Jones in 1958.

Oppy hits a bump in the road

▶ THE front wheel was wobbling last week at the headquarters of 'Oppy', the much-heralded $10 million film project about cycling marvel Sir Hubert Opperman, as the production team and its travel agent warred over $24,000 worth of unpaid fares.

Travel agent Juanita Scott said the debt dated back to November 1992 and the money was still owing after a mutually agreed deadline expired. "It was first-class travel both overseas and in Australia for Clayton Sinclair and Ken Lyons, the two producers," said Ms Scott, of Juanita Scott Travel. "They have been duckshoving me for months."

Mr Sinclair, of Sinclair-Lyonos Pictures, told Spy a line of credit was being established. "We were like many other businesses, hit by a couple of bad debts which held us up, but Juanita is a friend and I am upset that she has had to wait."

Mr Sinclair assured Spy it was all systems go for 'Oppy' which is scheduled to go in to production in October and to cinemas in the middle of next year.

FAX FROM Sue to Bruce, 8 December 1994

I had a long talk to Greg Coote this morning. He is in Kuala Lumpur making more millions for Village Roadshow. He was very chatty.

I said I thought it would be very good for the three of us to sit down and discuss the script and the financing/timetable and the line we should take with casting (this will determine budget and possible buyers) before you get fully engrossed with *Last Dance*. Greg agrees. We could do it next week, if I can get on a plane, but it may be best to wait till the next set of revisions are in hand.

Chris and Melinda very efficiently acquired a copy of *The Women in Black* which was waiting for me here yesterday when I returned from an AFC Commission meeting. I started it last night and, while it spends a long time (and quite amusingly) setting up, is probably about to get going. We've just met Magda in Model Gowns. I'll finish it over the weekend and check out the rights situation. Talk to you about it next week. Is there no end to the women you went to uni with?

FAX FROM Sue to Bruce, 9 December 1994

Antonia Barnard, producer and currently Film Finances person working under my thumb, has just returned from Singapore. She brought back a coffee table book about Raffles, which has some excellent references in it. She says Singapore is unbelievably noisy and there's not much of the past left. Raffles isn't too interested in co-operating with film crews but might with our picture because it's historically based. In any event the interior of Raffles though 'restored' has changed a great deal and it might be better to recreate the rooms of the period accurately in a studio.

As Roadshow now owns practically the whole of Penang, they might be able to get us some good co-operation up there. I haven't given up on the possibility of filming on Sumatra either. These are just thoughts to be filed away for later.

The annual Christmas cake arrived yesterday, thank you. Gratefully received as always. Also got your postcard – the book about Kath Walker is not brilliantly written, but done with love, and very moving.* Kath deserves a more professional and comprehensive biography.

FAX FROM Bruce to Sue, cc Greg Coote, 9 December 1994

Could you come over next week? I'm going to Greg's party (on 16?) so you could come to that too!

As I wrote the script I thought of Judy Davis as Adrienne Pargiter, Elizabeth Hurley as Rosemary Leighton-Jones; Joan Plowright would be a great Mrs E. A. Roberts. Brenda Fricker could be Miss McAllister. There are loads of great actresses around. The one playing Susan must be superb.

FAX FROM Sue to Bruce, 13 December 1994

It's not too late to buy Henry Parkes' house, as no doubt you've already heard.

Attached is a letter from Betty fyi. I'm encouraging her interest as I think it's helping to keep her going. I've written back saying I'll send the revised draft down to her next week.

See also a copy of a letter to Greg Coote. Not a peep out of him today. I think they'll welsh out of buying me a ticket. Pity about Greg's party, too… You should ask Greg about Brenda Fricker, whom he seems to know. I'll get the next draft of the script to Alison Barrett so she can think about possible Australians. If Greg doesn't come through with the air ticket we should talk while you're in LA about strategy. I'll be

---

* It was a privilege to have known Kath Walker, Aboriginal poet, artist and activist. She worked with us on *The Fringe Dwellers* and played a small role. She was later to adopt a traditional name, Oodgeroo Noonuccal. SM

over there in February for the American Film Market, but I'd like to get the script out to be read before that.

The Women in Black. I've finished it, and thoroughly enjoyed it. Such a sweet and innocent little tale and didn't it bring it all back! As to would it make a film? I think it comes into the 'would anyone go to see a film about an old Jewish lady and a black chauffeur' category. It would all depend on how you handled it. Apart from *They're a Weird Mob*, no-one has ever tackled the post-war migrant experience on film, and it would be fun to do it. There's almost nothing left of Sydney in the fifties. Even where the buildings are still there, the attractively named *street furniture* blurs the landscape.

I think in your hands it could make a charming film and the period is only a problem to be overcome. I'm interested in how you would adapt the book. How did you come by the book? Did Madeleine St John send it to you?

FAX FROM Bruce to Sue, 14 December 1994

I'm meeting Greg on Friday at 4 pm to discuss the next moves. We'll call you from his office. He seemed very enthusiastic.

FAX FROM Bruce to Sue, 20 December 1994

Your proposal re the book seems fine to me. Let's see how they reply.

We probably shouldn't do anything on the *Captives* casting until some time in January – when I have the new draft (I hope).

I'm keen on Kerry Fox for Susan.

Have a great Christmas.

FAX FROM Sue to Bruce, 22 December 1994

Whoopee! The agent's agreed on the option for *The Women in Black.*

I do think it's a film we could keep control of. The budget should be small enough to attract investment without too many strings. We could cast a couple of hot European actors as Stefan and Magda, which would help with sales, without over-inflating the budget.

Re *Captives*, I certainly don't intend to do anything until we're all agreed after the second draft is done. Are there any famous old bags who could play Mrs Roberts? That accent is so important in her case. Next time you're in England you should telephone Shelagh Brown – once you hear her speak, you'll know *exactly*.

We seem to be ending the year on a bit of a high note. Let's hope it all goes as planned.

CHAPTER FOUR: 1995

Song of Survival

FAX FROM Sue to Bruce, 9 January 1995

Women in Black. I understand you've been in touch with Tom Rosenthal who says you and Maddie should be 'meeting this weekend'. Either she's in LA or I've lost you! I've sent a draft rights agreement off. I've left you out of the agreement, removing the necessity for you to have to sign anything. When it's ready to sign, I will do a letter to you confirming your involvement, in case I walk under a bus before the film is made. I think that's probably the easiest way to handle it, if you're happy.

Captives. Letter in from Betty this morning, attached. Perhaps, if you've got a minute, you could respond. It's an incredibly lucid appraisal from an 85-year-old who knows nothing about filmmaking!

As you will see from the attached notes, I'm getting Mike Lake (or one of his minions) to have a fiddle with the budget. I spoke to Herbert Pinter [production designer] this morning and gave him the script. He's going to take a closer look for me. It might be an idea, if Greg will pay, to take him to Sumatra and Singapore in May. The poor guy has just had *Tracks* collapse under him – Julia Roberts didn't like the script. I reckon she finally faced up to the fact that she'd be spending three months with a camel as her best friend and thought: *Oh, no.* I think they're going to see if they can resurrect it with Meg Ryan.*

---

* *Tracks* was eventually made in 2012 with Mia Wasikowska.

I promised myself I would make no further comments about the script, but looking at it again in conjunction with the budget, a couple of thoughts occurred. In previous notes I suggested that we lose the Roberts' scene in Raffles, meeting them at the docks through the eyes of the characters we already know. I still think this is a good idea. If this were to happen, in its place there *could* be a short scene in a bedroom where Dennis and Rosemary, knowing it's their last night together, make love. This would add poignancy to their restrained farewell on the docks the next morning. I'm not entirely sure if this is a good idea, but thought it worth mentioning.

Could we put a page in the front of the script after the title page, using the Shelley quote?

> Music, when soft voices die,
> Vibrates in the memory
> Shelley

I really think it's important to sell the film on the music, as that's what grabs everyone.

I hope you all had a lovely time and that Katherine made a heavenly bride. We stayed in Sydney, read books, saw *Once Were Warriors*, gut-wrenchingly excellent, and *Quiz Show* which was great. Also saw *Shallow Grave* with Kerry Fox – gruesome but quite entertaining, if ultimately silly.

FAX FROM Bruce to Sue, 10 January 1995

I'm in London till Friday as I had to appear in *This Is Your Life* re Edward Woodward last night.

The budget looks okay though it might be tight to do it in eleven weeks. I'd have thought twelve to fourteen. I feel we'll lose (crucial) authenticity if we shoot in Queensland. Unless just the two camps are shot there and all the stuff outside done somewhere in South East Asia.

I don't think we need a love scene between Rosemary and Dennis. It's poignant as it is, also, they leave on the night of the party at Raffles – no time for a quick bonk. They're a refined English pair, not yer Aussies.

I agree Kerry Fox is a better actress than Nicole Kidman, though Nicole was much better in her Australian films.

(I enclose the letter I wrote to dear old Betty.)

FAX FROM Sue to Bruce, 12 January 1995

Women in Black. Tom Rosenthal's response to the agreement was incredibly laid-back. I have to say Tom has been great to deal with, and seems very nice to me. Any residual charm you can expend on Maddie to oil the path won't go astray.

Captives. Thanks for writing so nicely to Betty. She will be so pleased. I'm attaching a letter in from Helen Colijn. I do love our prison camp ladies. I hope a) that I live as long and b) that I am as feisty as they are.

In regard to the budget, what I'm trying to do at the moment is to get into it all the things I know have to be paid for (such as your correct fee) without frightening the horses. I'm pretty sure we can get another week's shooting out of the contingency (which is nearly a million dollars) and the rest can be fine-tuned when we have a distributor on the hook and we know where we're going to film. Asking Mike Lake's opinion is really just being nice, for which I'm so famous.

FAX FROM Bruce to Sue, 12 January 1995

I'll try to have the revisions finished by Monday. Trish can then retype and Fedex a new script. I leave for LA tomorrow.

I don't think Madeleine's agent will be a problem.

I'll give Helen Colijn a call from LA. I liked her a lot – in fact all the old dears were pretty impressive.

See *Princess Caraboo* – a good script and very amusing. Well cast, although the girl in the lead (Phoebe Cates) isn't really great.

FAX FROM Sue to Bruce, 16 January 1995

Today I went to the film vault to throw out *Black Robe* – we have run out of money to pay the storage. Danny Tegg (who is intellectually disabled) runs the huge film storage facility – four storeys with about a squillion feet of film – with military precision. He knows where every frame is stored. It's great to see how much confidence he's got since he's been doing it. He loves a chat and told me several funny stories about George Lucas and Steven Spielberg and pitched me an idea for a movie. When Tony Tegg sold the vault he sold Danny with it. What an asset!

FAX FROM Bruce to Sue, 16 January 1995

I'm sure the 50th anniversary of the end of the Pacific war will bring a surge of publicity. What a shame we'll have to release the film the following year!

It's Virginia's 50th birthday on 21 January, though judging by a phone conversation yesterday she doesn't want to know about it – she has cancelled a big party she was having.

FAX FROM Bruce to Sue, 18 January 1995

You might be getting a call from an actress called Beatie Edney. She's English, very nice, and played Pierce Brosnan's wife in *Mister Johnson* (the best reviewed film I ever made by far, and seen by no-one). She recently had a role in *In the Name of the Father.* I'm not sure why she's going to Oz but am told she might be looking for some work.

The UK video release of *The Getting of Wisdom* has been held up, the company claims, by their inability to find any colour pictures for the box. I was wondering if you could contact George Miller (Noddy), *not* Dr George Miller, who was the stills photographer on the film and see if he could locate anything. Could Roadshow in Sydney have anything on their files?

The revisions on *The Captives* are *much* more extensive than I imagined. What with all the notes I have from you and changes of my own it's turned into a big task. I'm working on it fairly hard, every spare minute, as I'm anxious to get it back to you before I have to plunge 24 hours a day into *Last Dance.*

See *La Reine Margot*, largely for the performances of the male actors and Virna Lisi, though I suppose Isabelle Adjani is effective.

Virginia disagrees with me over my suggested casting of Judy Davis as Adrienne on the grounds that 'I'm always casting glamour queens'. She wouldn't accept my argument that I don't regard Judy as particularly glamorous but a good strong actress! It's very odd what other people regard as beauty. I know many people who think Jamie Lee Curtis is gorgeous, something I find impossible to understand. Yet Virginia is obviously being quite serious as I recall when I was doing *King David* she was urging me to offer Judy the role of Bathsheba.

PS. Avoid *Natural Born Killers* and *Mrs Parker.*

FAX FROM Sue to Bruce, 19 January 1995

Will look after Beatie Edney in our quaint antipodean way.

Am trying to track down Noddy, no easy task. But we're on the case...

I'm not surprised that the *Captives* work is complicated, but in a way I'm pleased because it's got to be so deep, and it sounds like it's happening. I'm sure it's going to be great.

I wouldn't class Judy Davis as a glamour queen. But we *have* to have a bit of glamour, first for those distributor *blokes*, and then for the paying public. As long as they can act as well.

PS. Found him! He was a little bemused but is working on it. He said *Cinema Papers* did a spread so we'll try them tomorrow.

FAX FROM Sue to Virginia, 19 January 1995

Nice to hear from you. I suppose you get withdrawal symptoms when Bruce goes away and the Samson fax flood goes with him. It's certainly full on at the moment, with *Captives* and negotiating *The Women in Black*. BB says he'll be free in August to start *Captives*, so I'm pushing him to finish the script so that I can start driving Greg Coote mad to get the financing done. I think I'll have the next draft in about a week, I think it will be quite a lot changed from the first one, given the groaning that is going on about getting it done.

Give my love to John. I wonder how he feels about *Little Women*? I sent him a note via Sarah Radclyffe that *Sirens* is going into the Istanbul film festival (where?) but I don't know if he got it.

FAX FROM Bruce to Sue, 19 January 1995

Lyrebird Rising sounds very interesting and I'd like to read it.* Greg Coote recently sent me *Patrick White Letters* which are fascinating.

I'll be gone from here next Thursday. I'll send you the Nashville address.

Keep me posted on the *Wisdom* stills. It just shows how important it is to keep tabs on these things. I recall that the SAFC had lost virtually all the *Breaker Morant* stills/negative/colour slides even by the time of its foreign release in 1982.

---

* Given Bruce's love of music I thought he'd be interested in Jim Davidson's biography of Australian Louise Hanson-Dyer. SM

I don't know how I'm going to go on this revision of *The Captives*. I really need more time than I have available, but will do my best. I think your analysis of the script's structural defects is entirely accurate. I believe I know what must be done, but the actual doing of it is complex because of the range of characters. I've spent the last couple of days sketching out a new structure for the middle section – but of course this means quite extensive changes throughout.

I like *Quiz Show* too. The young lawyer in that, Rob Morrow, is in *Last Dance*. *Once Were Warriors* hasn't opened here yet. I saw *The Madness of King George*, which is very well directed (by the director of the original stage production) and beautifully shot and designed (Ken Adam) but seems to me rather one-note as a movie. However it's bizarre enough to hold the interest and the contemporary analogies are lightly stressed enough to be surprising.

FAX FROM Sue to Bruce, 20 January 1995

Bingo! We've found *The Getting of Wisdom* stills. At least we think so – Film Victoria think they have all the B&W and all the colour negatives. Chris is going to ask them what else they have for it and *Don's Party*. They *might* even know where the masters are.

As long as we get something good enough to show distributors for now, more work can of course take place after you've finished with Miz Stone.

I'm still slugging it out with Sarah Lutyens [UK agent for Madeleine St John] – I'm doing it myself instead of involving a lawyer, as I have a good pro forma contract and lawyers take forever and charge a fortune. It's more work but it's kind of interesting.

FAX FROM Sue to Bruce, 24 January 1995

I spoke to Sarah Lutyens yesterday and we have agreed all remaining points. I'll get the amended contract to her probably tomorrow. She sounded very nice, sounds like she went to Heathfield with Sarah Radclyffe.

I have *nine pages* of 35mm colour transparencies of *The Getting of Wisdom* and what looks like *all* the black-and-white negatives – about 70 rolls. I'd say the colour has been cannibalised extensively over the years. There are a few good ones, a lot of ones with people's fingers up their noses, crew in shot, etc. Let me know what you want me to do. We have to return the originals to Film Victoria asap. There are some shots of you directing in the buff (well, practically) looking extraordinarily young and quite attractive apart from the sideburns.

Helen Watts is on a mini series near Kobe – she's the third PM so far and took over a week before the earthquake. Says things were bad enough before it hit.

FAX FROM Bruce to Sue, 24 January 1995

Very good news about *The Getting of Wisdom* material. Tell George I'm enormously grateful to him or whoever tracked them down, though it's a bit mystifying as I know Jeannine Seawell [French sales agent for the film] has repeatedly requested stills over the past 15 years and never located any.

Let me know when and where you want the cheque sent on *Women in Black.*

By the way I'm leaving here Thursday for Nashville. I had a ghastly bout of flu over the weekend and did very little on the *Captives* revision, but today am working away; the changes are extensive and it's fairly slow going. I'm anxious to get through it because of the work on *Last Dance.*

FAX FROM Sue to Bruce, 25 January 1995

I can modestly claim almost the entire credit for finding the stills –

a flash of genius really. George suggested *Cinema Papers*, which led me to thinking about Film Victoria, the only state body which has been going uninterrupted since then. *Almost* equal credit goes to Chris, who did the chatting up and extraction.

FAX FROM Bruce to Sue and Greg Coote, 3 February 1995
Last Dance Production Office, Nashville

Despite the huge amount of work involved in pre-production for *Last Dance* I am going to make every effort to get the revised script to you by the end of February – there's a long weekend coming up and I'm hoping to do the bulk of the work then.

It is absolutely certain that I am totally committed to this project and have no intention whatever of letting any other film intervene. I have a few other projects in development, but everyone knows of my obsession with *The Captives*.

Greg, thanks again for *Patrick White Letters* which I found riveting. I knew Patrick White very well between 1960 and 1962 and am only sorry now that I never kept the innumerable gossipy letters he wrote to me between 1962 and 1970.

FAX FROM Sue to Virginia, 3 February 1995

Glad to hear the celebration went off successfully. I think 50 is really the hardest one of all to come to terms with. By 60 it will be 'Oh, what the hell'. It's remarkable how quickly one adapts, especially when faced with the alternative.

I had a long chat to B yesterday, he's been very bad about finishing the second draft of *Captives* – hardly surprising given he's four weeks from shooting another movie. However he swore on a stack of Bibles that *Captives* will be his next film and he won't take anything else in the meantime. So we will have to see if we can raise the money with one and a half scripts!

High drama here with timber workers blockading Parliament House for a week with trucks – everyone from the PM down had to walk in. The government completely stuffed up the renewal of the woodchip licences, resulting in the Greens and the timber industry at loggerheads (neat pun) with the government in a no-win situation in the middle. Into all that cantered the new leader of the Liberal Party, John Howard, who is the only one who can stand up to Keating in the House. Unfortunately Labor and Keating had become lazy and complacent when the Libs degenerated into a rabble intent on destroying themselves under poor old hopeless Alexander Downer. So politics will be a bit more interesting now.

FAX FROM Sue to Bruce, 6 February 1995

I think you should do the interview for Tony Buckley – he's bending over backwards to structure it in a way that you approve. And you wouldn't want all those other egomaniacs having the last word!

PS. Did Patrick White fancy you?

FAX FROM Sue to Bruce, 7 March 1995

I'm home [from Colorado], to incessant rain and humidity – sticky floors, damp towels, sweaty bodies. The drought has broken on the east coast, with floods along the coastal rivers up into Queensland. Everything is green again and I found a mushroom in Centennial Park. (Only one but we ate it anyway.)

The skiing continued to be excellent, with a dump followed by nine straight days of cloudless sunshine. The highlight was one magic morning on Aspen mountain with a group of gun skiers on powder snow zooming very fast from top to bottom with no-one else around.

I had five days in LA where it was also wet and quite nippy, with one of those continuous white skies that give you a headache. The American Film Market is a madhouse of buyers and sellers from all over the world all talking at once. I called on Greg Coote in his carefully underdecorated office in Century City to discuss *Captives*. He looked as if his personal physician had just administered Prozac intravenously, he was so laid-back. He feels we should wait now till you complete the second draft, but that should give us plenty of time to do a deal. The budget came out at about US$14 million, and Greg thought that that was quite manageable – even if it does go up a bit.* So I feel more relaxed now about the delay.

Thanks for sending the rewrite to date, and the notes. It's definitely on the improve, although there may now be a *touch* too much history lesson – something which will easily iron out when it can all be seen in context. The increased conflict in Act 2 sounds like what it needs, alongside deepening friendships and understandings between some of the women.

We put a deal together in LA for this low budget film I'm hoping to do called *Dating the Enemy*. I need to earn some money and it's a very good script by a young filmmaker called Megan Simpson, who will also direct. The shooting all takes place in Sydney, so I'll be able to bounce all the other balls at the same time. It may not happen, we have to cast it yet and Megan has to do a rewrite, so we'll see.

I don't know if I told you that we have rented the building next door to the office at Pyrmont. While I was away (cleverly timed) we cut two holes through downstairs in Chris' domain, and pulled out the dividing fence and laid a courtyard. It's going to be great. Twice as much space, and the dogs *love* the bigger garden. You'll be able to have your own office next time you're here.

The state election is coming up so Bob Carr is slugging it out with John Fahey. They are both promising the film industry more money so we're a bit impartial. Paul Keating is having a public slanging match with Kerry Packer which is bound to end in tears.

---

* In fact the budget ended up being $25m, funded by Fox Searchlight Pictures and Andrew Yap.

FAX FROM Sue to Bruce, 16 March 1995

I've heard from Sarah Lutyens that the option money for *Women in Black* has been received.

Also I heard from Greg that he was sending the first draft plus notes of *Captives* to Fox. I organised a tape of the music from Helen so I hope he sent that too. Haven't heard from him since. I had a nice letter from Betty this morning enclosing the text of an interview she did in 1986 with Crawford Productions. Her writing is getting a bit shakier. She thanked me for my card from Aspen and said it reminded her of her skiing trips to Switzerland in the fifties.

I guess you've started shooting and so I hope it all goes well and that the picture is a big hit.

FAX FROM Bruce to Sue, 17 March 1995

We've just finished one week's filming on *Last Dance*. The material looks okay and the actors and crew are all fine. Though you never really know anything until it's all put together and often not even then. If I had seen the rushes or early cuts (or any cuts) of *The Piano* I'd have predicted oblivion for everyone involved.

Greg called and said he wanted to send out the first draft of *Captives* to a few people. I wasn't too keen, but he seemed to think it wouldn't do any damage and he wants to see if something can be done before I do the revisions after the shoot of this film.

Tony Buckley's crew arrived here yesterday and did interviews with both Jack Thompson (who is playing the Governor of Tennessee) and myself for Tony's Aussie film documentary [*Celluloid Heroes*]. I'm still not at all keen on those things but it seemed childish to refuse Tony, who I've always admired.

Virginia is going to Sydney early April to look at yet more houses. I can't stop her moving back to Sydney and have been trying to persuade her that we must sell the London flat as the cost of maintaining it while we're not there would be untenable. She doesn't agree, but can't give me any convincing reasons for keeping it.

Do you know an Australian composer, Ross Edwards? Lives at Pearl Beach. *Major* stuff. Could be good for our score.

FAX FROM Bruce to Greg Coote and Sue, 22 March 1995

Great news that Tom Rothman is interested in *Captives*. It'd be ideal from my point of view if we could pin down some kind of a deal at an early stage – mainly so that we could work out a schedule for ourselves. If they (Fox) insist on it (e.g. the prison camp portion) being shot in Australia I'm sure it would be possible. I'd still like to do some of the early scenes in Singapore.

I know there are some special effects sequences but I'm certain these can be handled well in Australia provided there's an allowance in the budget. I think firstclass model work is the clue for some key shots in the attack on the ship. I saw a documentary on *True Lies* and there was a hell of a lot of model stuff. I'll get on to the script revisions as soon as the shooting of *Last Dance* is over.

FAX FROM Sue to Bruce, 24 March 1995

I guess we have to kowtow to your genius for getting a positive result from Fox on a first draft…

I asked Herbert Pinter if he thought the camp sequences could be shot in Queensland and he thought they could, subject to having a look around up there. I imagine Fox would be happy if we *based* the film out of Australia, did part of the filming here and got the necessary production values by shooting in Singapore, etc. We have a quote on doing the ship sinking with models/computer FX and it is the only way to pull off something so ambitious.

It would be good for you to give us a timetable to set up the picture which you would like – taking into account completing *Last Dance* and the opera – and any other little events we don't know about; then we would have something to work towards with the financing. And I could plan my life.

I *had* heard of Ross Edwards. I have to agree, his music is extraordinary. Some of it is extremely beautiful. Some is a bit modern for my liking. But I think he could give us a lot of emotion in the score, plus the necessary tension.

I'm halfway through *Patrick White Letters*, which I gave to Tom for Christmas. What a pity he wasn't born about thirty years later, he'd have got so much more out of the Sydney of today, rather than that philistine era after the war. But he wouldn't have enjoyed Centennial Park half so much, now it's crowded with predatory cyclists and patrolled by jack-booted rangers. I don't think that Satyajit Ray to direct *Voss* was one of your most practical ideas but I'm sure you had your reasons at the time. A few years later and you might have directed it yourself. I am constantly reminded of you when Patrick White talks about a new book, saying he doesn't know if it's any good or not. You have that reaction to your work in common.

We had the state election here on Saturday. The result is still unclear but is shaping up to be a hung parliament – 49 seats each. No-one can quite believe it, as it's more or less what happened at the last election. Either side might still be able to govern with the help of the hyperactive Clover Moore, your local member. Whatever happens, support for the film industry won't suffer, as both parties are very enthusiastic about making films happen in NSW. And both seem to be behind Fox and Murdoch setting up a studio complex in the showground.

I hope Virginia has time for a drink at least, when she comes out. She will be utterly seduced by the weather, which is moving into its autumn perfection mode. I went riding yesterday – I don't know if I've told you the saga of my mare, her extraordinarily beautiful foal and the drought. Anyway the little foal is now weaned and running free with thirteen of its little contemporaries up on the tablelands, and the mare is living in hand-fed luxury out near Windsor. We went for a long ride down country lanes through bush full of bellbirds. Heaven.

Things are going badly with *Dating the Enemy*. Every time we get all the balls almost into the air one drops with a thud. It's so hard to finance these low budget films.*

FAX FROM Bruce to Sue, 1 April 1995

We've just finished our third week on *Last Dance*. Hard to tell what it's going to be like. The actors are good and Peter's photography is his usual phenomenal standard. We finish shooting early May and then there's a ten-day layoff before we go to India. I'll spend that time doing the *Captives* revisions.

My only other commitment is the opera [*Sweeney Todd*] in January 1996, in Portland. I could dodge out of this but it would leave them terribly in the lurch. What if we did some pre-production – locations, key casting, after *Last Dance* is finished in October and then shoot any time after March 1996?

FAX FROM Sue to Bruce, 7 April 1995

No need to cancel the opera – we wouldn't like it done to us so we shouldn't try to do it to them. I wonder if you can complete the second draft in the ten days in May? Am still waiting to hear more from Fox so I guess their response will indicate the urgency or otherwise.

We [Tom, Robert and I] had a most enjoyable dinner with Virginia last night then crashed the Jeffrey Smart exhibition opening. Wonderful pictures. Margaret Olley was there, standing in front of

---

* *Dating the Enemy* was directed by Megan Simpson Huberman and starred Claudia Karvan and Guy Pearce. It is a romantic comedy about a young couple who wake up one morning and find themselves in each other's bodies. SM

several very gentle and sensitive portraits of her. It was lovely to see Virginia, she seemed in very good form.

I have to go to the Cannes festival in my AFC persona. I have a few people to see and I want to visit my cousin in Surrey whose husband, whom we all adored, died earlier this year. So I'll be in London for a couple of days toward the end of May.

I've finished *Patrick White Letters*. They just got better and better. He inspired me to have another go at the Ellmann biography of James Joyce. I've been trying for years to get past page 30 and PW thought it was boring to start with, so I'm ploughing on and it *is* picking up.

Bob Carr won the state election. Rupert Murdoch and Kerry Packer are locked in an incredible fight over the TV rights to the Rugby League, making millionaires out of all those neckless neanderthals whichever way it goes. There is no God.

Saw your star [Sharon Stone] on the Oscars, looking most unlike someone recently on death row.

FAX FROM Sue to Bruce, 2 May 1995

I had lunch with Greg Coote yesterday and he gave me the attached memo and script notes from Fox, which presumably you have already seen. As I understand it, Greg wants to be sure it's okay with you, then he will try and get Searchlight to commit.

We had Brett [Bruce's nephew and aspiring cinematographer] in here last week. He came in wearing a suit and tie a la his mentor. We gave him a whole lot of people to ring to look for work. Then we got him back a few days later to move furniture (for money). He and Adrienne Read's son Danny humped filing cabinets and a very tricky stationery cabinet down the stairs and out to the new back storage areas. They did quite a good job (the stationery cabinet defeated them). We will give him some other bits and pieces of work if we have them.

I just had a call from Nell van de Graaff to say her book is being published in Japan. She is terribly excited. I've promised to have coffee with her when she comes to Sydney.

We got all the money for *Dating the Enemy* committed last week – still a few hurdles to jump, but if we can tie up the loose finance ends I hope to have it finished shooting before you get here. Otherwise I'll hand it over to someone else. *Nothing* interferes with *Captives*!

FAX FROM Bruce to Sue, 2 May 1995

I don't see any conflict with the notes from Tom Rothman's group about *Captives* as they're along the lines of my own proposed revisions. I agree the music needs to come in earlier and that there needs to be stronger conflict. I believe I know how to achieve both these aims and will begin the second draft as soon as I finish shooting *Last Dance*.

Filming here is pretty exhausting but seems to be going okay. The cast, including Sharon, are talented. We have a brief shooting period in India at the end of May after which I'll be in London. I'd like to visit a couple of the Englishwomen who were in the camps. Could you send me the contact addresses again?

We can't use the name *Captives* as a film of that title was released last week.

FAX FROM Sue to Bruce, 8 May 1995

The notes from Searchlight seemed quite useful and suitably deferential, so I hope it all meets with your approval, and that Greg can get some sort of deal out of them soon.

I had noticed a film called *Captives* in *Variety* a month or two ago, but figured time would sort it out – as it now apparently has. Bad luck. What shall we do in the meantime – revert to *AVCO*? A title hiatus is a bore.

There has been a tremendous amount of publicity about VE Day, and I'm sure there will be more in August, for VJ Day – and of a somewhat different kind, as I think there has been bugger-all reconciliation with Japan. I now think we should prepare something and announce the film and get some publicity at that time.

Helen Colijn sent me a CD of the music recorded by a choir in Holland. There are some different – and very beautiful – pieces on it (all to Miss Dryburgh's arrangements) to the tapes we have, and the recording quality is fantastic. I've asked her for some more copies, so I can send you one.

FAX FROM Sue to Bruce, 12 May 1995

I've taped a documentary for you called *Eternity*, about the old man who used to write the word on the footpath. It's a quite beautiful film, which I think you'll enjoy for its own sake, directed by Lawrence Johnston, an AFTRS graduate. But it also has a score by Ross Edwards. It will be in your London goodies parcel.

I've arranged with Virginia to stay a night or two at your place after Cannes. I think you'll be in India.

FAX FROM Sue to Bruce, 16 May 1995

I had a meeting with Tom Rothman in Cannes on Monday. It seems to be looking good.

I spoke to Ken McKenzie Forbes on the phone yesterday about *Pearl Fishers*. I don't think he's got his act together apart from the possibility of getting the soundtrack down later this year. We could talk about this also in London.*

* This never happened.

FAX FROM Sue to Bruce, 2 June 1995

Greg Coote is here and we spoke yesterday. It seems that all is okay with *A Voice Cries Out* and Fox Searchlight. I understand Lenny has been involved also, so you probably know more than I do. But when Greg spoke to Tom Rothman he said he didn't mean to give the impression that he wasn't interested in making a deal now, and I understand that is going ahead – subject, as it always would have been, to the rewrite.

I had lunch on Wednesday with Clifford Werber from Fox, who is out here sniffing out the territory (Kim Williams was also at the lunch but I'll get on to that in a minute). Werber had read the script and was very enthusiastic about the film. They've all got their needle stuck on more music earlier and the internal flashbacks. But I don't feel any concern that these reservations won't be overcome when you finish the next draft.

So the bottom line, as always, is the revision of the script. I've sent you the music produced in Holland. If listening to that, and to Edie's tape doesn't get you in the mood, nothing will! Do listen to the tape, it's full of emotion, and love (of a very respectable kind) for Viv.

On the plane coming home I watched as much as I could stand of *A Man of No Importance*, the Irish film with Albert Finney, Tara Fitzgerald and Brenda Fricker. It's an incredibly boring and pointless film, but Brenda Fricker looks terrific, and would be perfect for Margaret Dryburgh.

Kim Williams is now the head of Fox Australia, responsible for getting the studios up and running. It seems things didn't work out for him at the ABC.

FAX FROM Virginia to Sue, 2 June 1995

I am counting on us hitting Oz in November, which will work in well with *The Leading Man*. Guess what – Jim Carrey's agent approached us… surely the least likely Robin, but I'm prepared to go along with it if he is! It's a long shot so we'll see what his reaction to the script is.*

FAX FROM Sue to Virginia, 6 June 1995

The house in Numa Street turns out to belong to Bruce Allan and Helen Stiles. I have been there over the years to parties, but always at night. It looks very different to how I remember it. It was a sparkling blue day when I visited so I saw it at its very best.

Positives: Stunning views, lots of land on the harbour side, although very steep. House in good order, doesn't need painting or plumbing. Good laundry off a well-designed, functional kitchen. At the end of a cul-de-sac so no passing traffic.

Negatives: It takes a long time to get down Louisa Road. The block of flats, while unobtrusive, *is* there and probably causes traffic congestion. (Parties?) The kitchen and one bedroom look directly onto the street. There is a carpark between but no privacy if people are walking by and feel like a snoop. (I snooped and saw Bruce Allan.)

There is a spiral staircase from top bedroom to main area and down to basement. Imagine getting down it at night to the loo without waking up the household or breaking your neck.

I took a roll of film of all the unattractive aspects, which I'll mail. I

---

* *The Leading Man* was written by Virginia and directed by her brother John Duigan. (Whatever Carrey's reaction was, the role was eventually played by Jon Bon Jovi.)

didn't go for the agent at all, I can see why you don't. Unusual, they are usually smarmingly charismatic.

I'm now keen to see how my report lines up with Kristin's.

FAX FROM Sue to Bruce, 12 June 1995

Attached are a few bits of interest. I'm sure you'll be amused by the Oppy story. Didn't we tell the silly old bugger? I'll be seeing David Parker on Wednesday, it'll be interesting to see what he has to say. He's already told me it wasn't all smooth sailing and money in the bank with Ken and Clayton.

Trust you received the CD safely. I've sent one to Tom Rothman also. Greg Coote was here last week and told me that Tom is proceeding to a deal – hopefully they will have something on paper this week. It will be subject to final script and casting, but what isn't.

Greg suggested we get together in London when you've finished the next draft. I would suggest the week commencing 24 July, which gives you six weeks from now. I must be here on 19 July, but otherwise clear at present so would like to set a time which I could then keep free, given the speed with which my diary fills up.

We've now set definite dates for *Dating the Enemy*, based around Guy Pearce's availability – shoot from 16 October to 1 December. It's later than I wanted, but it won't be a problem as I always find myself at a loose end from about halfway through the shoot, apart from looking at rushes and the odd bit of crisis management. It's all in Sydney.

Let me know your thoughts.

PS. The title!

Oppy fears he'll miss his life story

By RACHEL HAWES

CYCLING hero Sir Hubert Opperman has expressed fears he and his wife, Lady Mavys, may not live long enough to see his life immortalised on the silver screen.

The 91-year-old sporting star, former politician and diplomat jokes that it has been more taxing to make a movie about his life than it was to win the Paris-Brest-Paris cycling marathon in 1931 and film-maker Ken Lyons says he is inclined to agree.

The $10 million movie — which was hotly tipped to be an international success when it was mooted more than five years ago — has been plagued with creative and financial difficulties and producers at Lyons-Sinclair Pictures admit they are still searching for a screenplay and a cast.

Oppy — who became a household name in Europe after breaking 101 cycling world records in the 20s and 30s — said he and Lady Mavys were "a bit disappointed " that the movie was still on the drawing board when it was expected in the cinemas last April.

"I am aged and my wife is aged and we feel we will expire before it is made," Oppy said from his Melbourne home.

"It is a bit disappointing that it has taken so long but if a good film comes out of it at the end then the delay will be worth it."

Lyons admits that after three attempts to create a "magical script" the project had "gone backwards".

After a first draft by award-winning screenwriter Peter Yeldan was rejected in 1991, the producers then contracted the services of David Parker and Nadia Tass — highly acclaimed for the films Malcolm and The Big Steal.

Despite two further attempts at the script, Lyons said the hunt was on again to find a new writer.

Lyons said that "the scripts just haven't been right".

"They've lacked that sense of magic and we didn't want to go with something we weren't entirely happy with."

Oppy's legendary status as a cyclist started in 1918 after he took a job as a telegraph messenger in Victoria, which nurtured his love for the sport.

Some of his more spectacular feats included victories in the 24-hour Bol D'or road race, the Tour de France and the Paris-Brest-Paris race.

After retiring from international competition Oppy enjoyed a distinguished political career with the Liberal Party and later became high commissioner to Malta.

Lyons said although Oppy's story was an "extraordinary one", attempts last year to raise $8 million for the movie through a public float had been a "disaster".

"We knew that for investors to come into the project it had to be underwritten but just before the prospectus got on to the streets the underwriters pulled out," Lyons said. "We had heaps of brokers saying 'we have got money but it is not going to go into your project now it is not underwritten'.

"But the film is not in any financial trouble in the sense that we still have money to progress . . . and we are negotiating with financiers to bring the project to fruition."

Lyons said enough resources were available for "one more go at it" and he wanted the screenplay to resemble a "simple fable".

He hoped it could be completed by the end of this year so production could start and the movie could screen in cinemas before the end of next year.

FAX FROM Bruce to Sue, 12 June 1995

I still can't believe all that stuff about Ken and Clayton. It's been going on for years. How on earth do they make a living? What can be their source of income?

I have the Dutch CD. It's excellent. Probably worth trying to use that choir for the film.

I've just returned from the India shoot. Very very hot there – around 120 degrees Fahrenheit. Far too hot to go outside between nine and five. We shot only late afternoon and even then it must have been around 110.

I think that *Song of Survival* is the next best title to *The Captives.* There shouldn't be any problem using it, should there?

FAX FROM Sue to Bruce, cc Greg Coote, 16 June 1995

Thanks for yours on your new computer. New typeface. Quite nice. We have a new computer too. I still can't work it too well. I have heard on the news about the heatwave in India. Lucky you survived really. Should look great on film.

I would quite like to have our meeting over the weekend 22–23 July, which would be better for Greg seeing he has to leave for Australia on 29 July. Anyway let us know.

I don't believe there would be any problem using *Song of Survival,* in fact I think Helen [Colijn] would love it. Suggest we sit on it for a little longer and if nothing else comes to mind, I'll clear it with her. I agree about the Dutch choir, they would be great for the film.

Attached letter from Peter Yeldham fyi. Even David Parker was pissed off with them. David told me they are now talking to Rob George and his brother Jim. Rob is a writer from South Australia and Jim raised a bit of money during the 10BA incentives. There is no logical explanation!

PETER YELDHAM

TEL: (043) 511258
FAX (043) 531448
1102 Yarramalong Rd
Yarramalong 2259

Facsimile message. Number of pages
including this one

13.6.95

The Editor
The Weekend Australian.

Dear Sir,

I refer to an article by Rachel Hawes in The Weekend Australian of June 10th, regarding a film on the Life of Sir Hubert Opperman. Ms Hawes wrote, quoting the producer Mr Ken Lyons, that a first draft by me was rejected in 1991. This is untrue, as she could have discovered by checking her facts.

One of our leading film directors, Bruce Beresford, wished to use my script and direct the film, but Lyons-Sinclair, the producers, were unable to raise the finance. Mr Beresford was eager to take over the project and raise his own finance, and if he had been allowed to do so, Sir Hubert Opperman would certainly have seen his life story on the screen.

I'm afraid your journalist has allowed herself to be used in that familiar way chosen by unsuccessful producers, who excuse their own inadequacy by blaming the script.

Yours Sincerely,

Peter Yeldham O.A.M.

FAX FROM Bruce to Sue, 17 June 1995

I've been through *Last Dance* with the editor a couple of times and it's coming along quite well. After the end of next week there won't be much I can do to it until after the previews, when I hope the audience reaction tells us whether we have a film or not. All of this means that I should have time to do the rewrite, so that our meeting at the end of July will be fine. The only difficulties could come around if (a) I get stuck on the rewrite itself (b) Disney weigh in with lots of silly suggestions on the cut (c) I suddenly find, after a running of the film (which we haven't had yet) that it needs a hell of a lot more rearranging than I thought. Anyway I'm optimistic.

Beyond the Wire is also a good title. Maybe *Song of Survival* is better though. We'll definitely need to do some filming in Sumatra or Singapore otherwise we'll never get the atmosphere.

FAX FROM Virginia to Sue, 19 June 1995

Your photos arrived today – many thanks! Compared with the sullen grey of today's (and yesterday's, and the day before's) London, they look positively ravishing – even with the next-door flats!

What an excellent idea to take the worst aspects. Put against Miz Ghastly-agent's – you'd *never* know it was the same property. She managed to exclude the flats, the steep garden, the circular staircase (awful – I can't see B skidding down there), the ugly carpark and much besides. Not for us, I think.

B seems to have finished the editing... so there should be plenty of time for the rewrite. Encouragement and exhortations to be kept up from both ends!

FAX FROM Sue to Bruce, 22 June 1995

I have just spoken to Mrs Ailon Yeo, the Chinese lady who knew Margaret Dryburgh. Her father was in the Presbyterian church with

Miss D (not sure if he was a parson or not) in Swatow, China, and they all travelled to Singapore together in 1929, when Mrs Yeo was ten. They were together in Singapore until the fall. So I think worth a visit. She said, 'Oh, when I think about Miss Dryburgh I forget my angina. I am alive again.'

FAX FROM Bruce to Sue, 25 June 1995

I spoke to Lavinia Warner (who I'll be meeting in two weeks when she's back from holiday) and will call Shelagh today. I spoke to Jenny Greer, who lives in Chichester. She was in the camp for nearly four years. I'm going to see her on Tuesday. She sounded very sharp on the phone, though, like most of the others she said she's 'not in great shape'. She told me Vivian Bullwinkel had died. Did you know?

The editing on *Last Dance* is progressing well (God only knows who could sit through this harrowing film) so I'm finding some time for the rewrite.

FAX FROM Sue to Bruce, 26 June 1995

You should certainly call Shelagh, she'll know who you are I'm sure. Maybe you should do both her and Sylvia Cartner, who lives in the same vicinity. Sylvia is the ex-BBC lady, who spent a lot of time with Norah. Although maybe it wouldn't be much use at this stage.

I hadn't heard that Viv had died. She was alive when I spoke to Mrs Eaton Lee ('Blanchie') a couple of weeks ago. She told me that Viv had called one of the girls recently and her speech was getting better. But of course it could have happened since then. They all keep in touch with each other on a very regular basis. I've arranged to see Mrs Yeo at the end of July.

FAX FROM Bruce to Sue, 26 June 1995

I was going down to Chichester to see Jenny Greer this morning when she called, at 7.30, to say not to come as she's not well. I'd more or less expected this as Shelagh had told me she was in bad shape. I'm calling on the weekend to try to arrange it again. I'm also seeing Shelagh and Sylvia some time next week. Meanwhile I'm working away on the script, changing even the 30 pages I'd rewritten. I have a lot of notes and know the direction I want to take. Let's keep our fingers crossed.

FAX FROM Sue to Bruce, 29 June 1995

I hope you have a nice time with sweet Shelagh. She's almost blind, did you know that? But at least when I was there, very alert mentally. You can see the girl in the old woman, too, which will be helpful for characterisation. They are all so frail now. But I do think it is keeping them hanging on.

First AD. There is no-one here at the moment who is a star, but you know my inclination to use as many Australians as possible. I am hoping to have Caro on *Dating the Enemy.** It might be nice to have a woman as First on this one.

How about Hugh Grant!!†

FAX FROM Bruce to Sue, 3 July 1995

I went down to Dover today and met both Shelagh Brown and Sylvia Cartner. Poor old Shelagh is on her last legs and her mind was wandering a bit. She didn't tell me anything I didn't already

---

* Carolynne Cunningham, later First Assistant Director and producer for Peter Jackson on *The Lord of the Rings* and other films. SM

† This was Hugh Grant's unfortunately timed indiscretion with a prostitute in Hollywood.

know and couldn't answer many of my questions as she couldn't remember. Sylvia – an ex-BBC radio producer – gave me a one-hour taped interview she did with Norah Chambers a few years ago and it's very interesting and useful.

Editing proceeds on *Last Dance* and I have to show it to Disney on 2 August, in Los Angeles.

I'll try again and contact Jenny Greer tomorrow. The phone hasn't been answered for a week, though Shelagh tells me she talked to her last night, but she could be confusing last night with 1945.

FAX FROM Sue to Bruce, 5 July 1995

What a shame about Shelagh. She was entirely on the ball when I met her and coped quite competently with her incipient blindness. But at this end of their lives, the only thing that is surprising is that they are still here after all they went through. I'm glad at least that you got something out of Sylvia.

Don't kill yourself – we need the *body* alive and kicking.

FAX FROM Bruce to Greg Coote, cc Sue Milliken, 10 July 1995

Dear Greg

I could meet Nicole Kidman while she's in London, though with the combination of the script rewrite and the editing on *Last Dance* I'm busier than Mick Jagger's financial adviser. Let's see if the agent calls me.

PS to Sue. Do you know Williamson's house? Is it worth it?

[Handwritten note from Virginia] *Mum's the word on this one. It's* not *on the market and only offered to us. Love V.*

FAX FROM Virginia to Sue, 11 July 1995

The latest development on the housing front has rather thrown B into an apocalyptic gloom – I think he thought it (the move to Sydney) would never really happen, and this latest thing is kind of pre-empting the issue rather neatly. He's getting the house surveyed and valued. Meanwhile faxes have been flying to accountants and lawyers consulted and alerted.

Perhaps a little show of enthusiasm about the latest one might help mitigate his grumps… A pity about the road but the place itself is so special I feel it would probably exert a spell in the long run. It's probably as good as we can get for the money in that position.

Anyway if you feel moved to eulogise at all, don't hesitate!

FAX FROM Sue to Bruce and Virginia, 11 July 1995

This is an interesting development! The Williamsons bought that house the same year we bought Bondi, indeed we were at the same auction where we unsuccessfully bid on a house in Randwick. That's eight years ago.

I heard from Betty this morning – 'I hope Bruce can see Jenny Greer Pemberton. She was not a singer but good fun and a good friend to everyone in the camp.' She also says that Shelagh 'was an important member of the voice orchestra and a very musical person'. Too bad you got to her too late. Betty hasn't been too good so she's off to the Gold Coast for five weeks to get some sun.

FAX FROM Bruce to Sue, 11 July 1995

I spoke with Greg a few hours ago and assured him I'm still working away. It looks as if I'll be in Australia for a few days in August as Rob Morrow, my lead, is out there doing a Brando movie. I'll have to arrange to post-synch him in Sydney.

Williamsons called us and said they wanted to sell the house then called back and said they'd changed their minds.*

What do you think of the title *Paradise Road*? I believe I can work it into the script to give it some meaning. Most of the other titles sound either wussy (*A Voice Cries Out*) or TV-ish (*Beyond the Wire*).

FAX FROM Sue to Bruce and Virginia, 13 July 1995

I had a visit from Kristina Nehm [Trilby in *The Fringe Dwellers*] the other day. Last year she completed a degree in communications at Sydney Technical College and she's in a short list of ten writer-directors selected to make ten-minute dramas funded by the AFC and SBS. Her script is clever and funny. She's full of life and wit, and it was great to see her and to see her doing so well. She showed me a couple of short films she'd made during her course and they're not bad. Also, I don't think I told you that Bob Maza is now on the AFC Commission. I got him appointed to help promote the Aboriginal cause, and it's great to have him around. I saw Kylie [Belling, also in *Fringe Dwellers*], too, at a workshop in Melbourne recently. And Ernie [Dingo], of course, is a *star*.

FAX FROM Sue to Bruce, 18 July 1995

I've just spoken to Edie. She sent us a video of her being interviewed on TV a few years ago.

Somewhat trepidatiously I asked her how Viv was – although I knew if she'd died, Edie would have let me know. She said she's doing okay, battling away to recover her speech and to walk with a frame. Determined to succeed, which one expects she will do. So Jenny must be with the same pixies as Shelagh.

---

* Eventually they did buy the house from the Williamsons.

We've been invited to drinks on Thursday with Rupert Murdoch and the Fox crowd – schmoozing the film industry because of the Showground studio, I guess. I've just faxed Greg Coote asking for an update on the title, deal with Searchlight, etc. I'd prefer to know the answers myself if it comes up at the drinks.

When are you off to Italy?

I'm reading Marlon Brando's biography which is surprisingly enjoyable.

FAX FROM Sue to Bruce, 20 July 1995

I tried *Paradise Road* on Kim Vecera of Village Roadshow whom I happened to be talking to and she said it sounded like television! Didn't go for *Beyond the Wire* either. Maybe we'll end up with *Song of Survival* at the end of it all. *The Paradise Road*? I guess it depends on how you can work it into the script.

Don't come down between 5–12 August because I'll be in Perisher.

I'm going off to cocktails with Rupert Murdoch in a few minutes. (There's a few other people going too.) The showground studio is being announced today. Tom Rothman will be there. Tony Safford of Miramax is *desperate* to get a look at the script. But I guess you know that. He said $20m isn't too big for them.

FAX FROM Sue to Bruce, 21 July 1995

A glittering occasion at the Art Gallery of NSW last night. Everyone who is anyone around here was there to listen to Murdoch and Bob Carr announce the Fox Studios in the Showground. Murdoch is looking kind of old. I hope he lives long enough to see it through.

The place was swarming with Fox executives and I met Bill Mechanic and Peter Chernin, the CEO of Fox Studios, as well as Tom Rothman. The film was mentioned in the speeches as Bruce Beresford's *Beyond the Wire*, one of the films they are planning for Australia. Tom

Rothman was very friendly, and seemed very enthusiastic about doing the film. He told one of the other Fox execs the story, and seemed to understand it very well. I think they really want it.

If they don't, Tony Safford of Miramax does!

FAX FROM Bruce to Sue, 24 July 1995

I'm faxing an article from the *Sunday Times*. I think we've come across Phyllis Jameson, before – though I can't remember in what context. I've certainly not met her. The article is interesting, because absolutely all the other women I've spoken to who were in Palembang have insisted that, although they were treated very badly, they were not sexually attacked. In fact, my research has shown that sexual attacks by Japanese soldiers were very rare, at least on European women. There was a death penalty for it. I'm inclined to think that the ones that did occur (inevitable in five years of war) were well out of the ordinary.

I haven't heard again from Lavinia Warner.

I'm still working. I've dropped the nurses being massacred in the beginning. I think it's so shocking it will overwhelm the film. Also, although I'm making no attempt to whitewash the Japanese, it was not the norm but the behaviour of an isolated lunatic commander. It could be the subject of a film in itself, but will unbalance our choir story.

There were some interesting anecdotes on the taped interview with Norah Chambers.

Country Life has had very good reviews here. I'll see it late this week. I saw Phil Noyce's *Clear and Present Danger*. Brilliantly directed by him and beautifully shot by Don [McAlpine].

FAX FROM Sue to Bruce, 26 July 1995

I'm not sure we've heard of Phyllis Jameson – as Jameson is her married name. Lavinia Warner might have come across her. It's not clear what she meant by 'sexually harassed'. When you think about it, there are other stories of this nature – Edie's friend going off to service the Japanese, the Officers' Club the Australian nurses were forced to attend, the attempted rape in *Three Came Home*. It would have been remarkable if there hadn't been a bit of nasty business in all that time. But I'm pretty sure that what our ladies tell us is the truth – one of them would have spilled the beans for sure.

Yesterday I heard 'The Captives' Hymn' on my car radio! I was driving to lunch and there was a news report about 1000 ex-servicewomen meeting in Canberra for the end of WWII, and they sang the hymn. It was announced as written by Margaret Dryburgh who died in a POW camp in Indonesia. It sounded wonderful sung by so many voices.

You are probably right to drop the massacre. It would add subtext if you have the Viv character arriving late in the camp, with the story which they must keep secret or her life too will be in danger.

FAX FROM Bruce to Sue and Greg, 30 July 1995

So – here's another draft of the script. I have introduced the idea of the choir a lot earlier and then tried to introduce tension (and incident) by having various difficulties in the way of the first performance.

As you've seen I've used the title *Paradise Road*. I'm perfectly willing to change this to anything we all like, but I think it's quite colourful and has the advantage of not referring to the music. I think this frees up the film from the expectation that it's all about the music while I find it much more interesting if the music is only a key factor. I don't think there is any point in sentimentalising the effect of the music on the women, e.g. ending the film with them all singing in a blaze of glory and comradeship, but better to show it as an expression of their spirit. It couldn't and didn't save all their lives but what was amazing was that it happened at all.

I've changed a couple of the actual pieces sung. I think 'Bolero' is a good choice, partly because it should sound amazing for voices and partly because the incident where the camp, too weak to sing, actually beat out the rhythm is true (they did it when Norah Chambers left, not when Margaret Dryburgh died, but the latter is more effective dramatically). 'Country Gardens' which ends the film is a joyous piece, and should send the audience out with the courage and achievement of the singers in their minds and not the squalor of the final camp.

This is all a big undertaking but I'm sure a wonderful film could be made. I'll have plenty of time to refine the script further. I expect to do a lot of revisions after I've visited Singapore and Sumatra.

FAX FROM Sue to Bruce, 31 July 1995

By complete coincidence I just learned yesterday about a stage play on the subject of the Palembang camp, which has just opened at the Ensemble Theatre, so we went to see it last night. It's a two-hander, Melissa Jaffer and Maggie Kirkpatrick playing two survivors – an English schoolgirl and an Australian nurse, 50 years on. It's quite clever. They have been brought together for interviews for a documentary so they tell the story of the camp interwoven with an exploration of their relationship. It was written by John Misto. The performances are very good. I think it will do well in a modest way, and can only help awareness for the film.

FAX FROM Sue to Bruce, 1 August 1995

I do hate to be negative, but *Paradise Road* sounds like a B picture to me. Not that I'm crazy about any of the other titles, either. It would be nice to get a title which has a subtext to it and which would work into an interesting image with the women for promotion. That's why Greg likes *Beyond the Wire* – as a salesman, he can see the image.

We went to a concert last night, on the program was the first ever performance of Ross Edwards' 'Enyato III'. It could be good for the film. It's only about fifteen minutes long, but so beautiful.

FAX FROM Bruce to Sue, 12 August 1995

You ought to have the revised script by now. Sorry about the delay but I've been working hard on *Last Dance* and couldn't find time for the proofreading. Bear in mind that I'll still do revisions, especially after I've been to Asia, though I'm more convinced than ever that it'll make a wonderful film. It's probably still overlong, but it won't be hard to make cuts. I've done lots of, I think, subtle things, like having the nurses at the dance at the beginning instead of at the hospital. This is logical enough and enables me to use Raffles hotel as a microcosm of pre-war colonial society. All of that material is surprisingly accurate. I read in one (autobiographical) book of a British soldier bursting into a colonial club, up country from Singapore, and telling the diners that the Japanese troops were five miles up the road. They refused to believe it.

A budget of $15m (US?) is still very tight on such an ambitious project; I'm hoping it can be done in Australia for this amount. It would be nice not to be struggling too much.

FAX FROM Sue to Bruce, 14 August 1995

The script arrived shortly after we spoke. It *looks* impressive, 150 pages, must be some good stuff in there!

The title continues to get bad press. 'Sounds like a TV series' was a comment today – there was a soapie produced by Roadshow studios called *Paradise Beach* which was about blonde surfer bimbos lying about at Surfers. It only lasted one season. I'm coming back to *Song of Survival* as probably the best option. Anyway, I should shut up till I've read the script.

I was speaking to Ann Churchill Brown today (Judy Davis' Australian agent) and she said 'Judy was asking just this morning if I'd heard anything about the Bruce Beresford script'. So she must be keen.

FAX FROM Sue to Bruce, cc Greg Coote, 16 August 1995

I finished the script last night and it's amazing. You've done a tremendous amount of work and I do agree with you that that's the story – either a distributor will commit on this draft, or they don't want this film. It's a great read, moves always forward while giving a strong and complex understanding of what it was like. It's never boring and often very funny or very moving. I've got some comments about some of the detail but they can wait till there's time to talk. I understand that Greg's got some notes and we should talk when we've got those.

I think this draft, apart from the extra length, is a bit more expensive than the last, but the concept hasn't really changed, so I'm sure the logistics can be restructured to fit the budget without compromising what goes on the screen. The budget that I have at the moment is A$19m. It's based on eleven weeks shooting plus three weeks second unit for visual effects. I think you mentioned at some point twelve weeks, which is more realistic. But I figure we can do it in twelve weeks main unit and three of second unit.* Plus the computer-generated shots. Adding all this in will I believe still keep us in the ballpark.

I understand you've had some amazing offers but I do hope you will stick with this. If you take another picture now, I'd say it's curtains to this one. After three years, I just simply couldn't keep my heart

* A second unit is a small crew that shoots without actors – landscape, action, backgrounds for visual effects – to save time and money.

in it because I'd know there will always be something else first. And *you* would have to write to all the women and tell them!

I'm just off to the Movie Convention in Queensland, so I'll call you when I can.

FAX FROM Sue to Bruce, 18 August 1995

I spoke to Rose Pinter this afternoon who told me that Herbert is contracted until mid-February on a big B-picture shoot in Brazil [*Anaconda*]. I think an excellent alternative would be Roger Ford, who works for John Duigan. He also designs costumes. He did *Sirens* and is one of the best designers I've ever worked with. The great thing is he would take responsibility for the total look, sets and costumes.

I hear Rob Morrow walked from the Brando picture. I guess you won't be coming down.

FAX FROM Sue to Bruce, 22 August 1995

I reread the script on the weekend. I've made a few notes of comments of detail, but there seems to be little point in detailing them under the present circumstances.

Could you work 'The Captives' Hymn' in somewhere?

My only real criticism, one which I suspect will fall on deaf ears – is that you have been too hard on the Australians. The nurses – even Susan – do speak in yobbo language much of the time. In the Raffles scene they talk and act as if they are in the other ranks' mess. Only officers would be allowed into Raffles.

My other slight concern is that Alfred Uhry will rewrite the script in American. At the moment it is culturally very true, and it will only work if that intrinsic truth underpins whatever dramatic points are added. Should Alfred get a CD and *Women Beyond the Wire* (the book)? Let me know if I can help there.

It turned incredibly hot here over the weekend, and we have had the longest period in Sydney without rain since records began.

FAX FROM Bruce to Sue, 22 August 1995

I'll upgrade the Aussies' dialogue when I do the next rewrite. I don't think it's too bad. Alfred Uhry isn't doing another version of the script – at least as I understand it. I spoke to him on the phone after he'd read it and he spoke very highly of it. He said he couldn't improve the dialogue and thought the characters were wonderful. He thought we could cut fifteen–twenty pages and he'd also let me have any other ideas that occurred to him. If we start getting into rewrite land the process could go on forever with the film never being made. I felt that Tom Rothman needed someone like Alfred to tell him the script was good and he should be happy enough if we cut it and do a bit of polishing. I'd have done that anyway of course, but this is the way they do things here.

I had dinner with Herbert last night. He'll be tied up on his film until February, so will be unable to do this one if we're shooting in March. He said Roger Ford was a good idea.

Fox love the title *Paradise Road*. So there.

I think I'll be here till 1 September. I'm meeting Mr Yap on Thursday night with Greg.

FAX FROM Sue to Bruce, 22 August 1995

Sounds great about Alfred. Excellent, in fact. I *was* a bit alarmed about opening Pandora's box, as you said, although I figured you could control it with him.

I'm getting a script to Phillip Roope, the location person I mentioned, and he'll read it in the next week. He's free after *Dating*, so if we go ahead he can do the survey with us and all the locations.

I don't finish shooting *Dating the Enemy* until 8 December, and I can't in any conscience piss off before then. But I can, of course, do preparation work. Another problem is that there isn't a unit runner, let alone a production manager or an accountant, available in Australia until after Christmas. I want to use Anne Bruning, the fantastic production manager on *Dating*, and she won't be free till we finish shooting. We are heading into one of the busiest periods ever, with about six Australian features shooting and the Gold Coast studios chock-a-block with series, soaps and features. Nothing will stop me doing *Paradise Road*, but any help you can give to delay a tiny bit would probably enhance my life expectancy.

FAX FROM Sue to Bruce, 25 August 1995

Attached, if you can read it, is an article about digital effects. Animal Logic is probably the company we should use – or check out first – if we do the work here.

That demon for detail Tom Jeffrey pointed out to me this morning that the Japanese planes which attacked the ship were probably Zeros, and MIGs were Russian. He liked the script a lot.

Dame Edna launched Microsoft Windows 95 in Australia yesterday, so I guess that means Barry's here.

FAX FROM Sue to Bruce, 27 August 1995

Without knowing what you and Alfred have discussed, it occurs to me that cuts could be made in the opening Singapore sequence. There's 28 pages before they go to sea, and that's a lot of screen time. Maybe you could shorten the Raffles sequence – cut the Roberts' scenes in the bedroom, and meet them on the wharf. Shorten the scenes with Adrienne and Rosemary. I think it would be better to do a hospital scene with the nurses. You could have them ordered to leave in that scene, which would make it clear how absurd it was and why they didn't want to go. It would provide a dramatic contrast to the frivolity at Raffles. It wouldn't need to be too elaborate. If I'm correct there was an overflow into tents at the end so a couple of tents, a few patients and a lot of mud and noise would be cheap and effective.

You could also cut the refinery scenes. I don't like to say it but they remind me of *Spyforce*. Even if it's done with the Beresford panache, it doesn't really have anything to do with *this* story. It's essential to have the introduction of Singapore, but the story should get going as quickly as possible, and it doesn't *really* get going until they arrive in the camp, however exciting and dramatic the lead-up has been. The ship is intensely exciting and important because the audience has to know what they went through before they were caught. But Singapore could be shorter.

Hope this is of some help. I hear the meeting went okay with Mr Yap.

FAX FROM Sue to Bruce, 30 August 1995

I think Chris contacted Trish to say that I'm guessing the sound editor you were thinking of is Penn Robinson, son of Lee.

Yesterday I met with another of the nurses, Pat Gunther. I belatedly discovered that she lives in Mosman. She is *devastated* by the John Misto play, as it portrays the nurse character as rather lower middle class – she swears and talks roughly. Without any prompting from me she made the point that the nurses in those days were very middle class and like Betty she said they just didn't swear – nothing prudish about it, it's just that was the way it was in those times. It hurts them dreadfully to see themselves portrayed incorrectly, because they still feel so responsible for the ones who died. It seems unnecessary to distress them when it doesn't add anything to the story.

She did tell me a story I hadn't heard before. That in the first camp there was a small, battered pedal organ left behind by the Dutch. One day some of the women carried it out into the road and Margaret Dryburgh sat down and played it. It was rather out of tune and didn't sound too good but Miss D thumped out a tune as an act of defiance.

She said that in the first camp the Japanese were fairly lax, and there was no problem gathering together in groups, until the Kempeitai took over and banned meetings. She slept outside the house in the first camp, and I asked her whether she was worried a Jap might jump on her. She said not at all, they didn't really fancy the white women (they were so much bigger than the Japs), and apart from the Officers' Club incident they didn't bother them. Of course further into imprisonment the women looked so dreadful that not even the Japanese were interested – and they were terrified of disease.

We are meeting Tim Wellburn tomorrow. I'm hoping to get him to cut *Dating*. He lost his job on *The Island of Dr Moreau* when director #1 [Richard Stanley] left. Frankenheimer brought his own editor.

FAX FROM Bruce to Sue, 30 August 1995

It certainly looks as if the film might happen. I've talked to Tom Rothman, Greg Coote and Alfred Uhry. I've also sent a fax resigning from *Sweeney Todd*, the opera I was doing in January.

I agree with most of your notes on the changes and don't anticipate any real problems in condensing the script and sharpening some of the conflicts. Alfred is enthusiastic, which will make it easier for me.

I take your point – the nurses were a refined bunch. I don't think they're too rough the way they are at the moment. Bett is based on my Auntie Betty, who was certainly middle class and of that generation, but still had a ribald turn of phrase. You probably noticed that between the first and second drafts I took out all the nurses' (very mild) swearing. My mother (also middle class with immense pretensions to refinement) would swear like a shearer once she'd had a few drinks or was angry. I think our ladies insisting on their good breeding are idealising themselves a little. A few of the old dears have told me that when the ladies in camp got into arguments or physical fights, among themselves, the language was dreadful. Virtually all of them were well-educated and middle class.

FAX FROM Sue to Bruce, 31 August 1995

Thanks for listening to my squeaks about the nurses. I'd like to show the next draft to Betty if the bumps are ironed out.

I've just remembered that story that Vivian told us about Mother Laurentia going after the Japanese to allow them to empty the latrines after one of her nuns fell in. It sounded pretty funny (if you weren't one of the ones who fell in), and might be played as such.

I *had* planned to squeeze in some skiing while you were doing the opera – now it looks like next year will be ski-less. But a small price to pay if we get to make the picture. It's beginning to sound exciting.

We've now got a full green light on *Dating*. Pandora (the distribution company) loves the script, and everything seems to be coming together. I wrote myself my first cheque this morning.

FAX FROM Sue to Bruce, 4 September 1995

Your postcard arrived looking as if it had been through a jumbo-sized mail muncher and the address was completely obliterated by water except for NS 009. Australia. But it found us! Quite astounding considering the Pyrmont post office delivers most of our mail to Harris Street and the garbage cans in the back lane.

Phillip Roope, our location manager, says you could film in Penang for Singapore, as some places are still there from the British. Very straightforward filming in Malaysia, he said.

I'm seeing Greg here on Thursday.

09/07/1995 17:31 0713706916 BERESFORD PAGE 01

FAX

Date 07 September 1995

Number of pages including cover sheet

FAXED

TO: ~~Tom Rothman~~
BRUCE

Phone
Fax Phone 310 369 2359
cc: Sue Milliken
61 2 692 8926

FROM: ~~Bruce Beresford~~
~~Flat 9, 29 Bramham Gdns,~~
~~London, SW5 OHE~~
~~ENGLAND~~
Sue

Phone (44 0171)373 2485
Fax Phone (44 171) 370 6916

REMARKS: ☐ Urgent ☐ For your review x Reply ASAP ☐ Please Comment

Dear Tom,

I'd like to talk to you about the actual shoot/release of PARADISE ROAD. I mentioned to you that I'm supposed to be directing an opera for Portland Opera, which will keep me busy for them for the whole of January 1996. I can still resign from this production & have in fact already told them this was probable but am now conscience-struck as it leaves them in the lurch on a production on which I've already been working, intermittently, for over a year.

It seems to me that if I spent January in Portland and prepared the film in February & March, plus the prior November & December (ie of 1995) then we could shoot April, May, to mid-June. The film could then be completed by the end of November. Wouldn't this be satisfactory?

Could you give me a call asap? I'm at the above number in London.

Regards,

Bruce

Sounds like Heaven to me! More time to get it right, too. As long as you don't take on anything else!! Hope they agree

S.

FAX FROM Tom Rothman, Fox Searchlight Pictures, to Bruce, 12 September 1995

Dear Bruce

Forgive me for not getting back to you last week, but perhaps you have already spoken to Greg. In any case, we all seem to think that it really is not a problem for you to do the opera in January. I believe we can still get the movie for the end of next year and I think you will feel better about it. I gather we worked out a deal with Alfred so hopefully everything is moving along. Call me if you need me.

All the best,

Tom

FAX FROM Bruce to Tom Rothman, cc Sue, 12 September 1995

Dear Tom

Thanks for your fax. I've told the opera people and they're thrilled I'm not abandoning them. I just hope now I don't make a hash of the thing. Films are a pushover compared to directing operas.

Thanks again for your interest and enthusiasm. I'm sure *Paradise Road* will make an exciting film.

Regards,

Bruce
[Handwritten on Sue's copy]: Sue (fyi) We must work out the choir stuff very early in the proceedings. Any response from Judy Davis?

FAX FROM Sue to Bruce, 14 September 1995

I spoke to Judy Davis' agent yesterday. She said Judy has read the script, would read it again but would probably wait for the next draft. It's impossible to tell whether that's coming from Judy or is just the agent playing games. I agree about the choir organisation. I'd like to put somebody on really early to advise on setting it up properly. It will be absolutely critical.

I hope it all goes well with Alfred. I saw *Apollo 13* recently and what made it so interesting apart from being very well made was that it was essentially *true*, and while they adjusted the structure to fit the movie format, they kept pretty close to the facts. This was also the case with *Schindler's List*. One of the things that makes films about real events work is that they remain as close to the truth as possible. I think that is very important for *Paradise Road*.

I heard yesterday that Brian and Jean Moore are coming out here at the end of October, to launch Brian's new book. So I'm going to invite them to dinner.

Robert has just come back from Tahiti, where it appears that by chance he was the first person to learn of the firing of the bomb. He said it was pretty wild for a while. Have you been reading him in the [London] *Independent*? Have you also been reading about the Demidenko affair?

FAX FROM Sue to Bruce, 19 September 1995

I spoke to Alison Barrett today who loves the script. She's keeping herself free. I told her we wouldn't know for sure for a few weeks, but she's longing to do it. I also just had a call from Rose Pinter, who said the film Herbert is doing is a little bit shaky due to the level of the Amazon. So he might be available after all.

I'm thinking it might work to take my current production office staff on to *Paradise Road*. The timing would work quite well and the production manager, Anne Bruning, is as good as anyone I've ever worked with. The accountant is not only amazingly competent, but he's also cute. Production accountants are not known for their charisma, admittedly, but this one is very easy on the eye.

I believe Alfred arrives any minute. I hope it goes well and that you incorporate all my notes.

FAX FROM Bruce to Sue, 25 September 1995

Sorry for not replying for a few days but I've been busy finalising post-synch on *Last Dance* as well as wrestling with Disney over some last-minute inclusions/deletions. We have some differences of opinion over some fairly minor matters and I've told them that as we disagree I'll only do what they want if clearly instructed to do so – so far I've heard no more from them. I've also been working with Alfred Uhry every day, though Helen [Bruce's sister] came over and we went to Wales for the weekend. Saw quite a good production of *Nabucco*, visited a Roman Fort, Dylan Thomas' house and a beautiful town called Tenby.

It's been interesting working with Alfred, whose lack of knowledge of the subject brings a clear eye. I'm starting a rewrite tomorrow – and there'll be quite a bit to do with both structure and dialogue scenes.

I know that all the old dears are very concerned about their image of themselves but I really can't be too concerned about that. It is, after all, an *image* of themselves. Not that they weren't a lot of the things they imagined themselves to be (loyal, humorous, stoic, etc.), but there must be another side of the coin, even if it isn't evident in Betty Jeffrey's book. (Alfred and I went through it this morning – it's admirable in many ways, but emotionally on a girl-scout level.) If the characters are presented on this level no-one will believe it – and with good reason as it couldn't possibly be psychologically true. I don't intend to turn them into angst-ridden maniacs or crazed lesbians but there must be believable human conflict. I just read a wonderful autobiography by a German woman who was in a Gulag (*Light at Midnight* pub. 1967) and much of what she experienced in terms of comradeship, loyalty, etc., was exactly the same as the experiences of our bunch. In addition, she was much more astute and honest in depicting the less happy moments.

I don't think you need worry about the accuracy of the film. I agree with your comments about this. Remember, in the draft you now have, *I haven't invented any incidents at all*. Every one comes from research. The only stretch, perhaps, is that the bit of Dr Satchell pulling out the gold teeth happened in the Men's Camp in Changi.

I doubt if Herbert Pinter's film will fall through. I think too much money is invested for them to be able to afford it.

Barry is here about to begin a new show. Jeff Smart is coming to London for an exhibition and Brian Moore is promoting his new book, *The Statement*. Saw an excellent French film, *Colonel Chabert*. Have you seen *Hotel Sorrento*? I hear good things about it.

FAX FROM Sue to Bruce and Virginia, 27 September 1995

It seems I'm becoming just a *touch* boring about the nurses. This will be the last on the subject.

Editors. We've just undertaken an agonising search for an editor on *Dating* as the director wanted someone unsuitable, and then by the time he wasn't approved, there weren't too many good ones available. We ended up with Marcus D'Arcy, who worked at Kennedy Miller for years, took over from Richard Francis-Bruce on *Lorenzo's Oil* and cut *Babe*. We offered *Dating* to Tim Wellburn who'd just been dumped from *The Island of Dr Moreau* when the director changed. He turned us down for a pissy little telemovie with John Sexton. I wasn't at all pleased. Then he rang this morning to say that the telemovie has been postponed to next year and his house has been burgled. So now he's in a state. I'm a bit annoyed with him at the moment, as I really wanted him to cut *Dating*, but I also feel sorry for the poor silly thing. I think Richard Francis-Bruce is a good idea – he *has* been nominated for an Academy Award, which never hurts. Probably the most creative editor here is Jill Bilcock, who cut *Muriel's Wedding*, *Strictly Ballroom* and *Evil Angels*. She is presently editing *Romeo and Juliet* for Baz Luhrmann, which I think is being shot in the US. She's always in great demand so if you were interested I could check her out.

I spoke to Rose Pinter again yesterday. The story is that they are planning to take that film back to LA and downscale it considerably. The director therefore might walk, and Herbert doesn't know if he would stay in those circumstances or leave too. It seems that he would like to leave and if *Paradise Road* was a goer he would come to us. But if it's not happening, he's reluctant to give up the pay packet.

Have you seen *Babe* yet? It's a must-see. It has a fabulous score by Nigel Westlake (a definite alternative if Ross Edwards didn't work out). *Colonel Chabert* was pretty good, I agree. Although Gérard Depardieu is so fat! *Hotel Sorrento* will probably win the AFIs, but it's a pretty wet year and I think the film is not all *that* great.

Robert McFarlane's photographic exhibition is really lovely. Some wonderful stills, including one of BB on the set of *Puberty Blues* looking about eighteen. Can it really have been that long ago? Three shots from *The Fringe Dwellers* and a couple from *Sirens*. There were crowds of people at the opening and Robert seemed really happy. The gallery is about two minutes from your house with a coffee bar, magazines and books as well. A nice place to have a coffee and a browse.

The Brett Whiteley retrospective is on at the Art Gallery, a huge number of his paintings which are pretty interesting. Although I think a lot of his best stuff is missing. There was a nice exhibition on there recently of paintings of Hill End by painters like Drysdale, Friend, Jeffrey Smart and lots of others.

FAX FROM Bruce to Sue, 27 September 1995

I've finished going through the script with Alfred and will start rewriting this week.

I haven't seen *Babe*, though there's a dull trailer playing for it in London. Everyone raves about the movie, though.

I can't believe I looked younger in 1981.

Brian Moore and his wife, plus Barry and Lizzie are coming to dinner tonight. Also Anthony Havelock-Allan, who is 91 and produced *Brief Encounter* (I think one of the silliest films ever made).

FAX FROM Sue to Bruce, 29 September 1995

Roger Ford is in England and I have a number and could arrange for him to meet you.

Richard Francis-Bruce is cutting a picture for Disney which opens in July called *The Rock*. I think Nick Beauman would be available because he's cutting a documentary, which is why we couldn't consider him for *Dating*.

I hope your celebrity dinner went well. I remember Anthony Havelock-Allan. He produced some good films in the sixties. Ninety-one! I wonder if I'll be going strong at that age. Barry should be out here at the moment, there are two amazing rows going on: one about the 'feuds of medieval proportions' in the arts community – attacked in a speech by Hilary McPhee, Chair of the Australia Council, and one about the judges of the Miles Franklin Award over the Demidenko affair. It's like a great dog fight, with fur and feathers flying. Barry would get enough characters for a whole new show.

FAX FROM Sue to Bruce, 6 October 1995

If everything went according to plan we could keep the *Dating* production office and the key team – PM Anne Bruning and her workers – and they could slip straight on over to *Paradise* once they've recovered from their wrap-party hangovers. The office is in the old Ross Wood studios in Paddington.

Any more thoughts about designers?

Dating is coming together very nicely. Locations are all inner city – Potts Point, Victoria Street, Paddington markets. We have a most attractive cast of young actors – Claudia Karvan, Guy Pearce, Lisa Hensley, and Arthur Dignam in a cameo. And we are just starting to pull together an interesting contemporary music score. So if the director can do it, it might be a nice little film.

Brian Johns is coming to dinner with the Moores. He's now running the ABC and used to be publisher of Penguin Australia as well as a reformed Catholic and a huge fan of Brian M's. They should enjoy each other.

FAX FROM Bruce to Sue, 6 October 1995

Saw Greg Coote last night and told him I have the next nine days clear for the rewrites. Alfred and I worked out fairly extensive changes.

Herbert Pinter phoned last night to say his film has collapsed, so he *is* available. I told him we don't yet have a definite go ahead and probably won't till around 10 November.

Finally saw Bill Douglas' *Comrades* – partially shot in Australia and quite awful – polemical, political stuff.

Burnt by the Sun I thought very overlong and sentimental. It was an imitation Louis Malle film but without the panache.

What is the 'Demidenko affair'?

Either Nick Beauman or Tim Wellburn would be fine as editor.

FAX FROM Sue to Bruce, 10 October 1995

Good news about Herbert. Sounds like the film collapsed while Rose and the kids were in flight. I think we should use Terry Ryan to do the costumes. He's working with me now and very on top of things and doing a great job. He did *Sirens, Muriel's Wedding, The Year of Living Dangerously, Gallipoli.*

I've just finished *The Statement* [novel by Brian Moore]. Unputdownable. He maintains the forward momentum very consistently. The final moment was a little disappointing, even though you knew it was inevitable. It was a bit like swotting a fly after all that build-up. Make a good movie if you built up the parts of the colonel and the judge, and threw the focus to their view of the hunt. Good roles to cast.

That boring old *Comrades*! I did the completion guarantee on the Australian shoot and in my experience Bill Douglas was a huge phoney who had everyone bluffed because they thought he was an *artist*. I liked *Burnt by the Sun*, a *Women's Weekly* Russian movie. And I saw *Carrington* on the weekend. I bet you hated that. It's flawed, but I really enjoyed it – until, as so often happens, the last couple of reels went on too long.

A 22-year-old called Helen Demidenko won the Vogel Award for an unpublished manuscript by a young author. The book was subsequently published and then a year later it won the Miles Franklin Award. It's a sick little story about the role Jews played alongside Communists in persecuting Ukrainians before World War II, and how Ukrainians were subsequently involved in the Nazi massacre of the Jews. The author had heard the story from her Ukrainian father and uncle and had researched it with her relatives.

It was hailed as a brilliant piece of multicultural oral history and praised to high heaven by people like David Marr, and the judges of the Miles Franklin Award included such luminaries as Leonie Kramer. The literary world was very excited by the brilliance of this young author. *Then* it was revealed that her name was actually Helen Darville, she was the daughter of ten-quid Poms and had never been near Ukraine in her life.

Literary confusion. *Then* it turned out that the book was full of plagiarisms, most notably from an obscure 1950s book about

Ukrainian massacres. There was also a bit lifted from *Gossip from the Forest* [by Thomas Keneally].

There were lots of red faces among the literary crowd, with those who hadn't praised the book gleefully taking the piss out of those who had. There was also a fair bit of comment about how the eligibility rules for the Miles Franklin Award are bent this way and that to suit the fashionable and the politically correct.

The book is an odd mixture of extremely well-written passages interspersed with bits that read like they were written by a 22-year-old university graduate from Brisbane.

All pretty bizarre, but great for the Saturday papers, as long as you weren't involved.

FAX FROM Sue to Bruce, 19 October 1995

I got your fax about completion of the script. Clearly interesting things are in the wind. Did I hear a rumour that you are writing another script at the same time?

I saw *Silent Fall* this week. Beautiful work with the boy, and good strong suspense in the middle. There were some odd script things on the way through though. It seemed that some of the plot throughlines weren't locked down tight enough. The cops seemed to be out to lunch most of the time. I enjoyed it though.

I think Brian must be here already, in Melbourne. We are looking forward to seeing them next week.

We start shooting *Dating* on Monday. This time I'm borrowing your line – *I really don't know what this one will be like.* Nice cast, nice script, nice locations, but how the body swapping will go is anybody's guess.

FAX FROM Bruce to Sue, 23 October 1995

I'm still slaving away on the changes to the script thought it's been a heavy fortnight for me as we've been doing the final mix on *Last Dance.*

The script revision is more complex than it seems. Cutting isn't so difficult but it's resulted in a lot of reshuffling so that valuable lost dialogue can resurface, usually in altered form, somewhere else.

I'm hoping to finish by Wednesday but this is now unlikely. I'll then Fedex the script to Tom Rothman and follow on myself to LA, hopefully en route to Sydney.

See *Land of Freedom* the new Ken Loach film.

FAX FROM Sue to Bruce, 30 October 1995

I dreamed last night that you delivered the script and it was fantastic and everyone was happy. I hope this is an omen and that everything went okay in LA last week.

Ann Churchill Brown rang this morning and said, 'I can't remember if we've had the conversation about Judy.' What's this about, I wondered to myself. Tell me anyway, I said. She said Judy liked the script and was keen to see the next draft. She suggested that Judy thought the part was not all that *big.* I said it certainly would be, but of course the film is an ensemble piece. Then she got on to the real reason for the call – 'I see in the press that you're talking to Nicole Kidman.' 'Yes'. 'Well if you're thinking of Nicole you have to talk to me.' I said we've only talked to Nicole in person so far. That'll give her something to think about.

I had a letter from Betty Jeffrey: 'I knew Pat Darling was upset about *The Shoehorn Sonata* – I told her not to let it bother her. We know the true story and that's all that matters.' Nothing wrong with Betty's marbles.

Dating the Enemy is going quite nicely. Megan is very together on set, and the rushes, at least, are quite funny. We are cutting on Avid with film rushes, so it's interesting to see how it works. It's great to be able to try things out in seconds rather than wait for the film to be chopped up manually. Claudia Karvan is incredibly beautiful, and Guy Pearce is handsome and funny. Caro is doing an excellent job on this one, and I truly think she could handle anything. In case your *Canadian* is not available.

FAX FROM Bruce to Sue, cc Greg Coote, 30 October 1995 London

Please advise me asap whether you're given to prophetic dreams. Maybe this was the first.

My script rewriting was interrupted by a two-day trip to LA to show Disney the final mix on the film. They oddly made no comment at all. In fact, hardly anyone was at the screening. Not so odd in retrospect. I don't think any of the heavies at Warners have seen *Driving Miss Daisy* to this day. They certainly never attended any of our initial showings. I don't know myself whether *Last Dance* is any good or not. I fear it's heavy-going and that the legal stuff in it is impenetrable. There is some very good acting though. They're not releasing it until next May and are planning to show it at Cannes. At least that's the current state of play.

I'm back on the script now and hope to have it finished and Fedex-ed to you in about a week. I'm still very confident that *Paradise Road*, or whatever it's called, will make a great film. I think I know exactly how to do it, too.

I'm going to Bristol next Saturday night to see Barry's show. He's touring England but I gather it's not going all that great. There is still a depression here, though it's not official.

The role we offered Judy is a big one even allowing for the story being an ensemble piece. Regardless of that, it's a *key* role. Anthony Quinn won an Academy Award in *Lust for Life* and was on screen for a total of seven minutes.

FAX FROM Sue to Bruce, 7 November 1995

Herbert rang today to say he's signed a contract with Columbia(?) – which takes him to next July, so that, as they say, is that. Bernard next?

FAX FROM Bruce to Sue, 7 November 1995

I guess Herbert is working on the 'bird in the hand' principle. Maybe Bernard is our best choice.

I'm slaving away better now that *Last Dance* is finished, bar titles.

FAX FROM Bruce to Sue Milliken, Tom Rothman and Greg Coote, 14 November 1995

So. Here is another draft of *Paradise Road*. I've reduced the length successfully, I think, which has made the story move more briskly and dramatically. Most of the comments about the previous draft – such as making Susan more central to some events – have been done and I'm pleased with the result.

I wrote a brief modern prologue and epilogue but then decided to scrap it. I'm still not so sure it's a bad idea as it related the events to our own time and told them from Susan's point of view. I think my main reason for not including them at this point is that the ending is so dramatic and the use of the choir so powerful that any further additions can't fail to be anti-climactic.

FAX FROM Sue to Bruce, 13 November 1995

Eureka! It's arrived. It *weighs* well, and I'm trotting off home asap to start reading.

PS. A copy of Helen Colijn's book also arrived today. Must be a good omen.

FAX FROM Sue to Bruce, 14 November 1995

Much to-do here this morning about the script. It seemed that Roadshow LA could not print out from your disk. Anyway Danny Read, our office miracle worker, managed to put it on the *modem* to LA, where it was received satisfactorily. All very high-tech. I'm planning to take Danny on the film as my personal assistant as we can't afford to keep him on full-time at Samson otherwise. So the picture better happen.

Having slept on it and thought about it up and down the Bondi pool this morning, I still think the script is great. The structure is well put together and the change from the second ship to the train works well. Now the move comes just where it's needed to start the third act, and is integrated into the flow of the story, rather than embarking on another movie, which is a bit how the ship sequence seemed. The train of course will be much more manageable logistically. The lead characters are now more focussed (which should cover at least one of Tom Rothman's comments) and the tension and drama are greatly increased. It's going to be a *fantastic* film.

FAX FROM Sue to Bruce, 17 November 1995

Greg and I met yesterday, and I had a conversation with Norman Stevens from Roadshow this morning.

Everyone is very enthusiastic. You will be interested to know that when Chris had finished adjusting the layout from your disk, it typed out in normal script layout at 111 pages. As a film of this strength will easily carry at 120 minutes, there is room for more material if and where it will work. This should make polishing the draft a pleasure, rather than an onerous task.

So hopefully Tom Rothman will see this as a draft to commit to, with any polishing to be considered a work in progress as we get underway.

FAX FROM Sue to Bruce, 24 November 1995

Ann Churchill Brown rang again so I told her that I had got the impression from her that Judy wasn't incredibly enthusiastic about the project and we have decided to look further. She got a bit of a shock.

I just spoke to Betty who sounds very alert. She was very pleased to hear the news about the script. We have the fall of Singapore on Wednesday, I hear.

FAX FROM Bruce to Patsy Pollock [UK Casting Agent], 4 December 1995

I think the big problem is to concentrate on the four leading roles – Adrienne, Mrs Drummond, Rosemary, Susan (she'll have to be Australian). A lot of the others are important but will fall into place, I feel, once we have the principals. It's so difficult to cast any film! Actors are always whingeing but the truth is there are a hell of a lot of films, TV, theatre productions chasing a tiny group of people. I can say without exaggeration that I've never made a film in which the cast came together without massive problems. When we did *Black Robe* (in Canada, in the winter) absolutely no-one wanted to be in it at all, regardless of money. We had tremendous difficulty finding any young actors willing to play opposite Sharon Stone in *Last Dance*, the film I just finished.

I'd like to meet as many people as you can dig up when I'm in London, especially any 'names' that are likely to go down well with American distributors.

If Kerry Fox is in London, I'd like to meet her.

FAX FROM Sue to Bruce, 6 December 1995

At Patsy's request we sent off a script to Brenda Fricker today. Patsy told me Brenda had read the Perth guys' script and 'thought it was shit'. She also suggested I take the character page out of the script as it describes Margaret Dryburgh as 55. Patsy said Brenda is actually 42 and is sick of being asked to play grannies.

Alison [Barrett] said to tell you that Helen Morse is interested in reading the script. Pretty amazing as she usually won't even read.

FAX FROM Bruce to Sue, 11 December 1995

We're back in Jakarta and have been crashing around a lot here. General feeling is we'll be better off for the Singapore/Muntok town scenes in Penang. I'll explain the reasons at some point – exhausted right now.

FAX FROM Sue to Bruce, 11 December 1995

I'll be flat out like a lizard drinking tomorrow, with an AFC Commission meeting and the AFC's twentieth anniversary party at which I have to make a *speech*.

Casting. I spoke to Alison. Jackie McKenzie is very keen. Wendy Hughes is in Australia, interested and will be in Sydney on your return and will meet. Rachel Ward said no to Mrs Tippler in what I gathered from Alison was a rather forceful way. Helen Morse has a script… I think we can put a fabulous cast together here if we can get a few luminaries at the top. A good idea for Oggi is Lisa Hensley, who is in *Dating*.

I spoke to Tim Wellburn and he is of course incredibly excited about the prospect. Peter James' agent wants *double* what we paid him on *Black Robe*! I won't lose him but I have to try to negotiate him down a bit.

12/14/1995 07:07 0713706916 BERESFORD PAGE 01

14-DEC-95 14:54 FROM: SAMSON PRO...CTIONS ID: 6126928926 PAGE 2/2

Sue from Bruce

FOX SEARCHLIGHT PICTURES MEMORANDUM

To: Sue Milliken
Date: December 13, 1995

From: Joe Pichirallo
Extension: x4449

Subject: PARADISE ROAD CAST LIST
cc: Tom Rothman, Lindsay Law, Claudia Lewis, Greg Coote, Norman Stephens, Donna Isaacson, Christian Kaplan, Roger Mussendon

Here are our current casting suggestions for PARADISE ROAD: Sue

ADRIENNE PARGITER

A (Helen Morse / Wendy Hughes?)

Meryl Streep – she'll never do it & would be wrong

Emma Thompson said NO

B

Annette Bening – I wouldn't do it with her

Judy Davis great actress

C

Miranda Richardson – N/A

Greta Scacchi N/A

SUSAN MACARTHY (ADD Kerry Fox / Jacq McKenzie)

Nicole Kidman – possible, but I'm sure she won't do it.

Jennifer Aniston – who she?

Julianna Margulies " " ?

Gwenneth Paltrow –

Joely Richardson – no like

Robin Wright – not Aussie

Susan must be Aussie

ROSEMARY LEIGHTON-JONES

Kate Winslet – Meeting her – she's not a beauty

Gwyneth Paltrow –

Elizabeth Hurley – possible

Catherine McCormack – BB doesn't know her

FAX FROM Bruce to Sue, 13 December 1995

Arrived here (London) 5.20 am, caught the train to the flat and finally got the central heating turned on. It's freezing here.

Patsy Pollock is good news and very organised. Met three women today and will see more all day for the next three days.

I've spoken to the lady in Holland and we're meeting on Monday.

Rachel Ward is a spoilsport, eh? Was she interested in any other role?

Survey went very well. It was all useful vis-a-vis the script and I'm sure Penang will suit us fine.

FAX FROM Sue to Bruce, 15 December 1995

Ann seemed to think that Nicole has been wanting to do an Australian film for a long time, she wants to work with Judy, and she wants to work with you. Ann thought she was going to call you (I said I didn't believe she had).

If we were to make an offer to both of them through Ann, there is a chance that they would agree to do the film. She of course made the point that Nicole can write her own ticket right now and there are no guarantees that she *would* accept. But clearly it is in Ann Churchill Brown's interest to get them to do it, and she would try hard to pull it off.

If they both agreed, you could perhaps rework the emphasis of the script so that it is clearly on the two of them, with Margaret Drummond as the essential third lead. This would satisfy Fox, and could be very dynamic casting.

Hopefully I can call Ann and make an offer on them both on Monday morning. She goes to Italy on Wednesday so it would be good to get it going before then.

FAX FROM Bruce to Greg Coote, cc Sue Milliken, 25 December 1995

I saw a number of excellent actresses in London, many of them household names in England and Australia, but probably little known in America. Certainly there is no problem casting all of the roles with really talented people – but the key issues are the four leading roles.

1. Adrienne Pargiter. I met Judy Davis and she seemed very enthusiastic. She likes the script and discussed it and the various ramifications of the story with perception and intelligence. With an offer I'm sure she'll take the role. I must say I was taken aback at her appearance. She is extremely thin and looks older than her true age.

An English actress named Juliet Aubrey would also make an excellent Adrienne. She's well known in England through the lead in *Middlemarch* and other series and TV films. She's 32 and very attractive in a brooding and rather mysterious way. She has that knack of suggesting, perhaps unconsciously, that a lot is going on below the surface – very valuable for this character.

Another way to go is Joanna Lumley. She's well known recently through *Absolutely Fabulous.* She doesn't have the mystery of either Judy or Juliet but is very talented. She is a forceful personality and this could be exploited for the role. She grew up in Malaya and understood implicitly the social structure and relationships in the story. She has the lead in a big Disney film [*James and the Giant Peach*] which is about to be released.

2. Margaret Drummond. I spoke at length to Brenda Fricker on the phone and she said 'of course I'll play it'. Though she would like to meet me first.

3. Susan Macarthy. I gather we haven't heard yet from Nicole Kidman. I met with Kerry Fox who is very keen to play the role. She is an outstanding actress, in my view. Played the lead in *An Angel at My Table, Shallow Grave, Friends.*

4. Rosemary Leighton-Jones. I've spoken to Elizabeth Hurley, who wants the part but told me she's producing a film 'until mid-April'.

Not surprisingly this is the easiest role to cast as there are plenty of beautiful young English actresses around, most of them, it seems, very talented. Perhaps the pick of the bunch is Jennifer Ehle, who is a big star at the moment as she plays the lead in *Pride and Prejudice.*

We should talk about an American actress for Dr Verstak – perhaps Anjelica Huston?

CHAPTER FIVE: 1996

Jodie Foster would prefer not to be here for the whole twelve weeks

FAX FROM Sue to Bruce, 10 January 1996

I just spoke to Ann Churchill Brown who says that the Kubrick picture [*Eyes Wide Shut*] starts for Nicole on 15 June and so she has to pass. She said she was sorry, and hopes to work with you in the future.

This will of course impact on the casting of the other roles and so Greg and I will be speaking to Fox tomorrow and I will be in touch.

FAX FROM Bruce to Sue and Greg, 18 January 1996

I think Fox's casting ideas might be getting a bit out of hand. I don't want to be a wet blanket but I've never shared the general euphoria over Jodie Foster. I can't imagine that she could play 'English' though I'm willing to look at *Siesta* in the desperate hope of being wrong.

I'm also dubious about Annette Bening, but she at least looks a bit more the rather classy English type Adrienne should be.

As you know I'm passionately keen to make this film, have already put in a lot of time and effort and am aware of Fox's concerns. At the same time, I know I couldn't make it work if I felt the casting was wrong and am now beginning to think either (a) we shouldn't go ahead with the project at all or (b) I'll hand it over to a director who has more confidence in being able to make it work with the casting the studio wants.

Jennifer Ehle is definitely too young to play Adrienne. She's 26. Juliet Aubrey is perfect for the role and I really don't see why we can't offer it to her. Both Jean Simmons and Glenda Jackson are reading the script.*

FAX FROM Bruce to Sue, 23 January 1996

A shame we haven't found anything for Joanna Lumley, who is exactly the type of person the film is all about. Isn't the problem that Fox have never heard of her? Despite *Absolutely Fabulous*.

Why do men give their penis a name? Because they don't like 95% of their decisions being made by someone they don't know.

One by one we'll lose them all unless Fox lets us start making some moves.

Don't forget the arrangements with the choirmaster in Holland. Also, get the sound guys to check the recording quality on the CD. I think it's too 'interior' for our use, but I could be wrong. We'll probably have to rerecord.

FAX FROM Sue to Bruce, 24 January 1996

The budget has come in at A$17 million, and I'm confident we can make the film for that. We had the call with Searchlight, and they groaned a bit about the budget but seemed to buy it. But then they started carrying on again about getting some names in the cast. Greg was terrific and told them that none of us could live with a non-Australian playing Susan. They moved on to Adrienne and mentioned again Annette Bening and Robin Wright. We both repeated what we all believe, that if the film is not culture-specific

---

* For the next fortnight there were interminable faxes about casting.

it won't work. It's fair enough that they want some names to help promote and sell the film, and it would be good if we could persuade them to concentrate on Rosemary, Dr Verstak and Topsy. I suggested to Greg (you may not agree) that Dr Verstak *could* be younger if they wanted someone more up-and-coming than Anjelica Huston. Could she be mid to late thirties?

Greg is going to meet with them in the morning, to discuss names and try to move things forward. It might be good if you could talk to them and repeat what you have already repeated many times – Susan, Adrienne and Margaret Drummond must be cast according to nationality and type and with the best possible actors if the film is to work.

FAX FROM Dan Read [Sue's assistant] to Sue, 7 pm, 24 January 1996

I have just had a very depressing conversation with Bruce.

He called me at midnight his time, after a very long conversation with Joseph Middleton. He said that he didn't want to panic you but he feels that it is all falling apart. That he is losing interest.

'I don't want Jodie Foster, or Annette Bening. Fox's suggestions are just simply ludicrous. I'd rather not make it with miscast people, it won't be my film if so. We are losing good actresses, I think that the "names" that we have suggested are fine and with the strength of the story they would be able to market the film.' – etc., etc.

He would obviously like to talk to you. He said that he will be leaving the hotel at midday his time.

Sorry.

Also enclosed is some correspondence that came through while you were in the air.

FAX FROM Sue to Bruce, 25 January 1996

I've sent off a fax to Greg telling him of your concerns and saying that we need to resolve the casting situation as quickly as possible. I do think if we can all hold our nerve it will work out okay, and I told him I appreciated the slightly tricky situation he's in with Fox.

I think Patsy P must have gone off to do *The Saint* for Phil Noyce – apparently the casting person who was doing it (inadvertently) walked under a bus.

FAX FROM Bruce to Sue, 25 January 1996

Fox's suggestions have been so capricious from the beginning that it's hard for me to believe they're serious about the film. They appear to want to cast entirely on whim and are completely swept away by someone whose name comes to their attention, however briefly, and are willing to ditch established and popular people in pursuit of the ephemeral. Toni Collette, for example (there are plenty of others), is known to them from one Australian film but Fox would be happy to ditch an actress of Kerry Fox's accomplishment and style in favour of Toni! We need an appealing leading lady to play Susan.

I saw *Richard III*, which is a very good film, but Annette Bening gives the weakest performance, which pales beside the other women, especially Maggie Smith, who is sensationally good (should she be Miss Drummond?). Joseph Middleton doesn't want to send me *Siesta*, in which Jodie Foster has an English accent, as he says it will only confirm my worst fears.

I think we already have a wonderful cast and that this film will sell because of what it is.

FAX FROM Sue to Bruce, 26 January 1996

Fox's position I guess is that for their $12 million they want to know they can promote the movie. The irony is that if we'd suggested

Nicole Kidman to them a year ago she wouldn't have been good enough.

I gather that Jean Simmons is interested in the role. That's good news if you think she can play younger, dumpy, self-effacing until called upon to emerge as a charismatic saint. I'll see if I can get a viewing of *How to Make an American Quilt* this week.

Enjoy the skiing and forget *everything* but the following advice: if you are up, you cannot be down.

FAX FROM Sue to Bruce, 29 January 1996

Anne and I just met with Mark Turnbull, a potential first assistant director. He likes the script and is keen to do the film. The word on him from a number of people who have worked with him (and this came across in the interview) is that he is a brilliant First, great at scheduling and strong on the floor. He must be good with directors or Gillian [Armstrong] and Jane [Campion] wouldn't want to keep working with him, but he's hard on other people, I think. Jessie bit him, but as her taste in bitees is capricious, this is no indication.

I hope the skiing was great.

FAX FROM Bruce to Sue, 31 January 1996

The meeting went okay with the Fox heavies. Evidently Annette Bening is interested and the problem seems to be money. I hear she did *Richard III* for $50,000 but she was only on that one for one week; we'd need her for twelve. Fox don't want to pay more than $200,000, so…?

FAX FROM Sue to Bruce, 2 February 1996

Big day tomorrow! Fingers crossed.

We are trying to work out priorities when you return, and I'm wondering when you *actually* leave Portland. Can you let us know?

Anne and I might fly up to Port Douglas with Herbert the week of 12 February, to look at the locations and get the art department started. They are a bit edgy about the time they have to build, given that weathering will be quite important.

We have had a request via VRP from Jodie Foster who would prefer not to be here for the whole twelve weeks to play Topsy, and wondering if she could be scheduled into a shorter period. I kind of sympathise with the request, and I'm wondering what your thoughts are.

Anjelica Huston's agent asked how long we would want her for, and I said we hoped to be able to schedule her into a shorter period as most of her stuff is in the hospital. This *should* be manageable.

FAX FROM Bruce to Sue, 4 February 1996

The meetings in LA seemed to go well. Sorry I didn't call immediately but I had a ghastly and lengthy flight back because of the ice and snow. The plane was diverted to Seattle where we were told we were going to Portland by bus. But then they put us on a small plane and landed at 6 pm, about four hours late. I couldn't get out of the airport – no cars were moving because of the icy roads. Finally I found a bus that went to a downtown hotel, very slowly, and I ended up with a long walk over slippery streets.

Anyway, Annette Bening, Jean Simmons and Kim Basinger all seemed fine and enthusiastic. It'll be up to Fox to do a deal with Annette. I set her mind at rest about the safety of Port Douglas for her children. Kim would be fine for Topsy, I think, and if they could do a deal she'd be worth having. She's southern (the way the part is written) with a great accent. Jean Simmons will be good for Miss Drummond. She's a fabulous old thing, utterly unspoilt. I asked her if she'd do it with a Durham accent and she said she'd be happy to learn it. She's a cockney and was taught to 'speak proper' when very young. Her beauty was obviously a passport out of the East End.

FAX FROM Sue to Bruce, 5 February 1996

I had a call from Joe Pichirallo [Fox Searchlight executive on the film] on Saturday to say that he had heard that the Kubrick film has been put back to August, so I have spoken to Ann C-B to see if there is any point in reactivating Nicole. She's checking. I gather she spoke to you about Judy Davis on the weekend. All a bit tricky.

I spoke to Roger Savage about the music. He said his wife loves it! He also said it was a pretty extraordinary sound – hard to believe at times that it's all voices. He wonders if it was recorded in a studio with multi-miking and the reverberation added later, or if it was recorded as 'one' sound, with natural reverberation from the environment. If the former, it would be comparatively straightforward to remix the tracks to give a more natural sound, with possibly overdubbing closeups after the film was edited. If it was recorded as one entity with the reverb in the master recording, it would be more problematic. But he thinks either way we could probably use the recordings.

FAX FROM Sue to Bruce, 6 February 1996

We finally heard back from the theatre company in New York that they won't release Roger Kirk to do the costumes. Very tedious of them. A script is going to Terry Ryan who was, as you know, Herbert's and my alternative choice to Roger.

Mark Turnbull said no when I called him. He is now committed to *Oscar and Lucinda*, so that takes care of *that* dilemma. I am trying to speak to Michael Lake and will advise you further when I have.

Some days things go better than others.

FAX FROM Bruce to Sue, 7 February 1996

It's a shame about Roger Kirk, but I guess there's nothing we can do. Costuming is a big job on this one. Terry Ryan will be okay.

I spoke to Joseph Middleton about the casting. He's been in touch with Joe Pichirallo at Fox but has little to report so far. He hasn't heard anything about Annette Bening but has heard on the grapevine that Anjelica Huston is interested but is awaiting an offer. Evidently Fox hasn't approached her yet! Can you egg them along?

I assume the Susan issue can wait until I'm back. I also very much liked a Sydney actress named Cate someone who Alison brought in to meet me.

The opera is now being rehearsed straight through. We move into the theatre on Saturday, so it's all getting close. A hell of a lot of work involved.

FAX FROM Sue to Bruce, 8 February 1996

A few items on the agenda today. Things are looking up, although there is no news from Annette Bening. However, the good news is that a) the deal with Andrew Yap has been finalised, and b) Fox have told us to go ahead and start negotiations with Anjelica Huston and Jean Simmons. I have spoken to their agents and we will be making offers to them tomorrow. Anjelica has read it and loves it and her agent said what a fantastic script and project. Jean Simmons' agent said she is mad about it.

Ann C-B rang yesterday, said she had had a proper talk with Nicole, who feels that the Kubrick film *may* go back far enough for her to do *Paradise Road*. Ann apparently told Alison Barrett that Nicole really liked the project and it was the one film she's wanted to do here, and she really wants to work with you. So there is genuine interest. As no decision can be made on Susan until you are finished over there, we have nothing to lose by it.

I think we have found a viable First Assistant. His name is Colin Fletcher, he's done some big pictures, has a good sense of humour and would do a good job. He's been in India and I more or less overlooked him, but I ran into him at drinks last night.

Fox think that Kim Basinger might send the wrong signals for Topsy, but I suggested that if you had a Kim Basinger who brought herself down to the agonisingly unglamorous characterisation required, it might make a great publicity point for the film.

Apparently Jodie Foster's agent wondered if we could get the role down to two or three weeks. I told Joe P that this would be impossible, and that it would be difficult to reduce Topsy in the way that Dr Verstak could be scheduled around. Am I correct, or is there a way you can see that this role could be reduced in time? She's at Raffles, on the boat and there all through the camp, even though no mention after page 99. I think you would want her there at the end?

Lots to talk about. Sounds like you're busier than Paul Keating's speechwriter so I hope you can fit it in.

FAX FROM Bruce to Sue, 8 February 1996

I've been busier than Lady Di's legal advisers. We had a complete run-through of the opera last night (piano only), which was attended by the head of the company, so they were all pretty nervous. Today is the day off, though I had to go and give a speech at lunchtime. It was in a smart hotel, but I've actually no idea who I was talking to. Just a group of well-dressed people.

We move into the theatre tomorrow and rehearse there. There'll be a lot to do with the addition of the full set (on two levels) plus the orchestra and neck mikes. I'm trying to work on the revisions as much as I can, but it's tricky. Left alone, I can do them in 3–4 days.

Joe Pichirallo called and said he's heard Annette Bening is waiting for the new script. I told him this is bound to be a delaying ploy, because (a) she was surprised when I told her I was doing revisions, and (b) I emphasised to her that the revisions will streamline and focus aspects of the script but will not be fundamental changes. Her character will be changed less than any of the others. I think she could be having problems with the lovely Warren and is probably debating the wisdom of ten weeks or so in Australia with her two children.

I've never thought the Kubrick project would go ahead (God, I hate his films; along with Hitchcock, I think he's the lousiest famous director) but Nicole could keep us in the wings for a long time while she tries to work out what Mr K is up to. I could certainly meet her in LA.

Your new potential First doesn't have bad credits. You could easily check him out with some people. No-one's used him twice, though that may not be relevant.

I doubt if the role could be cut to two or three weeks to suit Jodie Foster. They're all in the camp together so they can't just vanish. Possibly Dr Verstak could be taken off the boat although I'd rather she was there.

Might be an idea if Alfred Uhry comes to Sydney by 8 March. As I said, I'll do my best while I'm here. I'm certainly not spending my time chasing chorus girls around. I'm the monk of the Mark Spencer correctional facility.

FAX FROM Sue to Bruce, 9 February 1996

It sounds like your speech today could have been a campaign speech for the Liberal Party. Apparently John Howard's launch of the Liberals' Arts Policy yesterday was full of well-dressed wives of Melbourne businessmen.

I have been as busy as Fergie's accountant this week. What with an AFC meeting, keeping *Paradise Road* lurching forward, trying to encourage the editor of *Dating the Enemy* that a three-hour comedy may not be all that funny, and endless social functions in the line of duty wearing one or other or all my hats, I'm quite looking forward to the weekend – although I've a tribe of Milliken cousins coming to lunch on Sunday.

Greg called and it seems that Annette Bening is now open to an offer which Fox will make in the morning. Roadshow will also be starting on the negotiating circuit with Anjelica Huston and Jean Simmons. Once *that* is underway, and if it looks as though we will get Miss Bening to the starting gate, I'll begin on the English ladies.

I don't think we should take the Nicole situation too seriously. You are not going to decide on Susan until you are back here, so to meet her in LA loses us nothing. If she professes interest at that time, we can move quickly on her agent and if there looks like being problems, we will just move on.

I will try for you to meet Anjelica Huston in LA, if she's there. I just don't see how we could schedule her in the boat and in all the camp stuff if we are to shoot the boat in the early part of the schedule and the camps in sequence. I'm sure she won't come for the whole time, and would cost a mill even if she would. So if we want her, we'll have to get through her stuff quickly. We always talked about doing Dr Verstak this way (or I talked and you didn't listen). We will just have to see how flexible she is.

We are going to lock in the 29 April starting date.

In spite of your denials about chorus girls, you're not going to get much done on the script before you finish the show. Maybe if Alfred Uhry is locked in it will provide the necessary incentive to do the preparatory work – or you could be like George Johnston and Charmian Clift and we could take photos of you with two typewriters.

The First Assistant. Colin had his first job in film after working in TV as second assistant on a film of Tom's, and I have completion-guaranteed a number of films he's done, and I know he's very good. My only reservation is that you will look at me if he isn't perfect and say 'Well...?' But Anne and I have agonised over this and whatever we do there is a potential for it not working out. We think this is the right way to go.

Indigenous Film Initiative. The AFC has just funded six short dramas by Aboriginal directors, and they are putting out some publicity to promote them. They are gathering quotes of support from famous people like Phil Noyce, Fred Schepisi and yourself. You are going to say: 'The future of the Australian film industry depends on the development of creative talent. This new initiative by Indigenous filmmakers will make a valuable and long overdue contribution to that future.'

Let me know if you have any problems with this.

FAX FROM Sue to Bruce, 12 February 1996

I've spoken to Ann C-B who will arrange for you to meet Nicole in LA.

I confirm to anyone who might think that we opened the bar early on Friday night that in my fax to Joe Pichirallo on 9 February I was referring to an Australian actress called *Cate Blanchett*, not Kate Winslet, as a possible contender for Susan if there's no go on Nicole.

Do bear in mind that if you could cut down the characters in the script – and especially the imported characters – it would help the budget a *great deal*. Bringing in so many actors means that the Australians get a huge minimum wage as they get an extra loading for each imported artist, and we have twelve at present count.

FAX FROM Sue to Bruce, 13 February 1996

Please don't try to apply logic and common sense to Actors Equity. The two are a contradiction in terms. I'm afraid that in spite of my Panglossian optimism, they are as impossible as ever. Unfortunately the alternative is to make the film under SAG [Screen Actors Guild of America] which is much more onerous. But the main reason for cutting down a bit on the cast is the sheer cost of getting them all up to location and feeding and watering them for such a long period of time. The extra loading is only part of the problem. I know we can't do the film with three people, but it would just help a lot to pull back a bit.

FAX FROM Bruce, 14 February 1996

I spoke to Joe Pichirallo a few minutes ago. He's still waiting to hear back from Annette Bening's agent re the offer. Evidently the offer made to Anjelica Huston was turned down derisorily, but he still thinks (can't imagine why) she might come around. Evidently she won't meet me in LA next week unless an acceptable offer is made.

I was in the theatre until 2 am this morning trying to help sort out their massive technical problems. We have a full run-through with orchestra on Thursday night and a dress rehearsal (with 3500 schoolkids) on Friday.

FAX FROM Sue to Bruce, 15 February 1996

The lead casting is like pulling teeth. We are just plugging on here, not much else we can do. We are about to have a budget conference with Joe Pichirallo. This picture is *extremely huge*. I don't want to bother you with it too much until you return, but we are going to have to be a bit artful to contain the costs.

Thanks for the new opening. I wonder if Susan should allude to the fact that the nurses *were* working their tits off by the time of the fall, with all the soldiers being chewed up by the Japs, so they needed the light relief of dances. Otherwise all we see is her talking about dances and then having fun dancing. It's not too sympathetic, the audience might think it serves them right to be shipwrecked, drowned and incarcerated.

FAX FROM Sue to Bruce, 22 March 1996

Rachel Griffiths has withdrawn. Seems she is auditioning for a lead in P. J. Hogan's (*Muriel's Wedding*) next picture which conflicts.

I am in negotiation with Ann C-B for Judy Davis. Judy is sick today so it might take till next week to sort out.

Actors Equity are being difficult about the English roles but I think it is political posturing and we will get around it – we have to.

FAX FROM Bruce to Sue, 22 March 1996
Los Angeles

I landed here about 11.30 am and went through the longest immigration lines I've ever seen. Virtually all Japanese. Since then I've been hard at it – and doing quite a bit of work as well.

I see Glenn Close tomorrow, for lunch, on the set of the movie she's doing. This isn't too satisfactory but she claims she has to fly to New York on Saturday so can't see me then! (Not putting in much effort for someone who's flown across the world just to meet her.) Jean Simmons is now on Sunday.

Rachel Griffiths won't be that hard to replace, though she'd have been a good Bett. Any word from Greta Scacchi? There's an English actress here, Cherie Lunghi, who I've worked with before and who is very talented, and she might be available. I'll call her and check. Do you want me to phone Judy Davis? If so, say the word and send the number.

I can't believe Actors Equity. You no doubt remember I expressed grave doubts about shooting the film in Australia when we first discussed the project on the basis that they wouldn't give a bugger that it wasn't exclusively about Australians and wasn't set in Australia. You lectured me at length about how reasonable they'd become. Ha!

I'm supposed to be seeing Joe Pichirallo tomorrow, though the lunch with the imperious Glenn could now stuff that up.

Alfred Uhry professes himself very pleased with the script.

FAX FROM Bruce to Sue, 24 March 1996

I've been busier here than Lady Di's divorce lawyers. After a lot of mucking around I finally spent quite a bit of time with Glenn Close; the confusion wasn't her fault – she was filming and under the delusion it was about to be finished. Anyway she seemed very pleasant – focussed and smart. Her hair is very short (I have photographs) and we both think the best thing is for her to wear a fall in the opening scenes (for the 1940s style) and then to lose it by my finding in the script a place where it can be cut (a lot of them cut their hair very short); that way we can go back to her own hair, though she'd need to let it grow from what it is now as it's too well shaped.

I spoke to her about the accent. She knows a good voice coach in London for the English accent but I said we'd try and find one in Australia. I spoke to her about weight loss/shooting in sequence, etc. She mentioned a doctor in LA who she knows has advised actors on losing weight in other movies. I told her we'd send her copies of the BBC tapes of Norah Chambers being interviewed. Would also be good for the accent.

I spoke at length this morning to Frances McDormand (for Dr Verstak). I knew her already and she'd be excellent. She's very enthusiastic. She evidently has lots of offers because of *Fargo* but is most enthusiastic about *Paradise Road.*

Jean Simmons has a very bad cold so we spoke on the phone only. She sounded terrible. She also is very enthusiastic about the whole project and the new script is on its way to her.

I hope things are being smoothed over with Equity. They were a major reason I left the country to work abroad in the early 1980s (after they forced me to fold up my project *The Break*) and I was hoping (assured?) they'd changed.

I am absolutely for casting all the Australian actresses we can in the various English roles but if the accents aren't credible we will have no film. I'm also aware of the economic considerations, but we can't come all this way and then ruin the ship for a half penny of tar.

****

This ends the correspondence. Bruce returned to Sydney and pre-production began in May 1996, followed by filming in September that year. *Paradise Road* was released in 1997 with the following leading cast:

Adrienne Pargiter	Glenn Close
Susan Macarthy	Cate Blanchett
Dr Verstak	Frances McDormand
Daisy 'Margaret' Drummond	Pauline Collins
Rosemary Leighton-Jones	Jennifer Ehle
Topsy Merritt	Julianna Margulies
Mrs Dickson	Wendy Hughes

Sue Milliken, Sydney, 2016

ACKNOWLEDGEMENTS

Our thanks to all at Currency Press, most particularly to publisher Claire Grady for a great relationship through the complications of turning this correspondence into a book, and to Melanie Ostell for enlightened and constructive editing.

Helen Trinca was supportive and helpful, as were Don Groves and Ron Tandberg in obtaining permission for some of the newspaper clippings. Thanks to the *Australian*, to Peter Yeldham for permission to publish his letter to the *Australian* and to David Stratton for his article on the AFI Awards. Also to Village Roadshow and Joel Pearlman for use of material relating to *Paradise Road*.

Special thanks to Tony Buckley, Al Clark, Clive James, Margaret Pomeranz, Rachel Ward and David Williamson for reading the ms and giving us the benefit of their thoughts.

Roberta McNamara, who took over from Chris Gordon as majordomo at Samson Productions/Film Finances, has been unfailingly patient and helpful in digging us out of technical holes and finding things which seemed to be lost forever.

And finally, our thanks go to the amazing cast of characters who worked with us, helped us, entertained us, drove us crazy and above all gave us the material for our faxes; they were bigger than any movie.

Sue Milliken & Bruce Beresford,
Sydney 2016

INDEX

www.ingramcontent.com/pod-product-compliance
Lightning Source LLC
Chambersburg PA
CBHW040305170426
43194CB00022B/2906
* 9 7 8 1 9 2 5 0 0 5 6 6 0 *